MICHAEL CORDÚA + DAVID CORDÚA

with JOHN DeMERS · photography by JULIE SOEFER

Cordúa

FOODS of the AMERICAS

bright sky press
HOUSTON, TEXAS

A NOTE ABOUT INGREDIENTS:

The folowing items that we use can be found at specialty Latin or Asian groceries. We often shop at Fiesta and HMart in Houston. Online, you can check www.amigofoods.com.

Achiote oil
Aji amarillo paste
Caldo de pollo granules
Chiles de arbol
Cotija cheese
Filé powder (Louisiana staple)
Guajillo peppers

Hon dashi
Hon dashi fish stock granules
Lime Dashi Juice
Matouk West Indian hot sauce
Panca pepper paste
Panela cheese
Ponzu citrus soy sauce

Powdered caldo de pollo
Smoked cotija cheese
Smoked panela cheese
Spanish chorizo
Xingu Brazilian beer

bright sky press
HOUSTON, TEXAS

2365 Rice Blvd., Suite 202
Houston, Texas 77005

Text and Photography Copyright © 2013 Cordúa

ISBN: 978-1-939055-49-1

10   9   8   7   6   5   4   3   2   1

Library of Congress Cataloging-in-Publication Data on file with publisher.

Thank you to Steve Campbell of Three Dots Pottery in Houston for sharing the plates pictured throughout the book.

Editorial Direction, Lucy Herring Chambers
Creative Direction, Ellen Peeples Cregan
Design, Marla Y. Garcia

Printed in Canada through Friesens

Thank you

for teaching us that
to love is to serve.

Dora María Cruz de Cordúa

TABLE
Of Contents

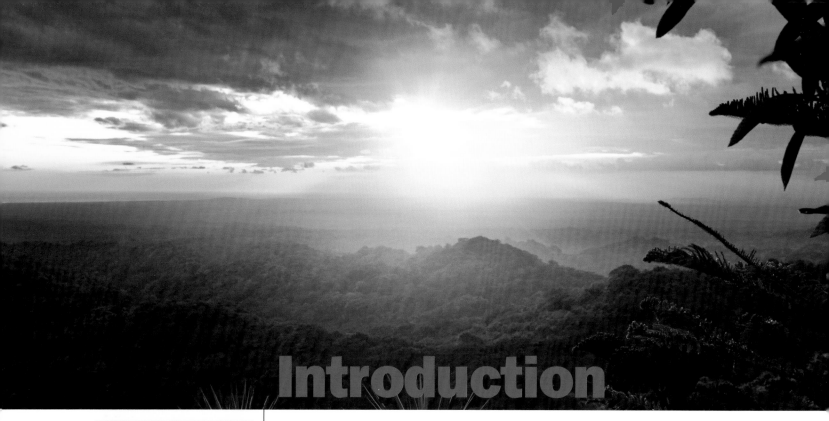

Introduction

> ## Our future is not a condition forced on us by our past. Nor are we held ransom by our perceived limitations.

I have always thought of myself as fortunate, but reflecting on my twenty-five year restaurant journey has magnified that feeling profoundly. Remembering the dishes and discoveries, the people and the places that I have been able to experience brings my understanding of this good fortune, and my gratitude for it, soaring to newfound heights. Though the destination seems obvious now, the path meandered through cultures and industries. Holding on to what is best about my heritage and opening myself to the adventure and knowledge of other countries kept me moving forward in what has turned out to be an exciting, meaningful—and delicious—life.

Growing up in Nicaragua gave me a worldview that no other place or time could have. The country of my youth was by no means a culinary melting pot, but it provided a backdrop and reality that allowed my imagination to run free. My life has been shaped and defined by my family, culture, time and place. The expectations my family and my country's culture had for me did not include cooking. The horizon my education and early career directed me toward had no restaurants. Beginning my career, I could not have imagined owning even one restaurant, much less seven, nor could I have conceived that my son would join me on this wonderful journey. Despite its culturally entrenched ideas about a suitable future for a young man, I thank Nicaragua for providing the space for me to discover these possibilities.

In that traditional society, ruled by social and cultural dogma, I was in many ways different. While I initially struggled to be free of these boundaries, now I wonder if that lifestyle actually provided the keys that unlocked the cuffs and allowed me to follow new currents into uncharted waters. Today, I am filled with energy and an unlimited capacity to love life, much as I was as a young expectant father.

Gathering these recipes and telling this story with my son David has provided a joy that is hard to express. His capacity to create and entertain is a blessing and an inspiration to my family and to those who share our work. It is our hope that what we have collected here will provide you with a taste of the delight we have experienced in a life rich with food and hospitality.

If I were an artist, I would want to fill my canvases with bold, vibrant strokes of color punctuated with surrealistic images, both real and creations of my imagination. If I were a poet, I would hope the pages of my journals would groan under the weight of the passion poured into them. If I were a singer, opera arias would mix with rock & roll, jazz and samba. Though I admire these artists and their passions, I am simply an explorer and a cook. Food is the medium I use to show you who I am. Sharing these recipes with you is the next leg of my voyage. These are familiar waters now, made more exciting and new again by having my son as first mate at my side. Together we offer you the best of who we are and what we have: recipes that provide a window into our hearts and express our deep desire to delight you.

I have been called a pioneer of Latin cuisine. I have even had the honor of being compared to Julia Child by people who believe that my work did for Latin food what hers did for French. But the food we provide, the food I affectionately call *ours,* did not come straight from my Nicaraguan heritage, or from any one region. It is an amalgam, like most of us are today. Our food was born of my need to create dishes that are an unbounded juxtaposition of Latin flavors, ingredients and technique, ultimately experienced as something never before tasted. This way of cooking came from my desire to take the ingredients of the Americas and meld them as an alchemist might. It was and continues to be unique, to me, to David and to those who have joined us to cook in our restaurants because they believe in the experience these dishes provide. Rather than an interpretation of any specific cuisine, country or region, we want to present you with

> It is up to us to visualize, create and give birth to our vision. This is my calling: To have the faith to believe, the courage to act and the passion to make it happen.

Never lose the sense of wonderment and curiosity. There is always something new to learn, someone new to meet. Never let this escape you…life is limitless.

a creation that is audacious in its originality and that embraces you with what we like to call Cordúality!

We will never stop seeking far and deep, pushing tirelessly against boundaries and perceptions. Our spontaneity in the kitchen is part of our very being. We seek three essentials in every meal we provide, at our restaurants and at home: It must be Latin, it must be artistic and, above all, it must be...YUMMY!

We have created this book for you with the hope that it will allow our food to become a part of your life. We want these tastes, these dishes and these presentations, so full of our heart, to delight you again and again. If we are gluttons, it is in our insatiable desire to create food that will be insatiably desired. Here is our story, the journey that has taught us to value and create such yumminess. We have worked hard to ensure the recipes that bring you to our table will work well in your kitchen. Make them with your family and friends, and come back to see what new discoveries we are making as our exploration—of food and life—continues.

With a heart filled with gratitude for our yesterdays together, I am forever,

Cordúally yours,

Michael Cordúa

Believe in your dreams—they exist in a secret, magical place just waiting to be unlocked. It's in our dreams that we are set free to be the person most true to our heart. Ignore the cynics who might silence you.

The Journey To
FOOD

The name Cordúa is Spanish, yet there are no precise records of when this strand of the Cordúas arrived in the New World. They migrated to Nicaragua in Central America by way of Ellis Island in New York and, perhaps foreshadowing where their journey would lead, through the port of Galveston in Texas. Records do exist, however, that indicate Cordúas arrived in the Americas from Italy and Germany. Without the ability to prove or disprove any specific theory about his ancestry, Michael Cordúa has pieced together some intriguing ideas.

The family name that seems so Spanish doesn't seem to exist in Spain. As is common when people move from one culture and language to another, the name refers to the place they believe they're from—in this case the Moorish city of Córdoba in the Andalusian region. Throughout history, Spain and its culture have been heavily influenced by the Arab world, to the point that cultural imports from North Africa now seem classically Spanish. Along with Sevilla and Granada, Córdoba was a treasure city of Moorish architecture, Moorish learning, Moorish literature and Moorish music, including the intense guitar and dance style known around the world as flamenco. Michael's ancestors seem to have emmigrated from this culturally rich country to other parts of Europe long before Columbus inadvertently introduced the Americas to the civilized world.

Like most traditional Latin families, the Cordúas have been Catholic as far back as family records and recollections go, but bits of family history hint at an earlier narrative. In 1492, when Columbus embarked on his first voyage, the Spanish monarchs under whose flag he sailed regained their peninsula from the Moors. As a result, they felt empowered enough to further secure their country and culture. They began practices, now known as the Spanish Inquisition, which forced non-Catholics to forfeit their goods and seek a new life in countries such as Italy and Germany. Many of these people were Jewish.

"It's fascinating to wonder whether this boy brought up totally Catholic in Latin America—educated by Jesuits, no less—might have come from a family that was Jewish when it abandoned the Spanish city whose name became our own," says Michael.

Latin America is one long swagger southward from the Rio Grande to the Patagonian ice floes near the South Pole. Up and down this long region, for almost a thousand years, Europeans have met and mingled with indigenous people. When the Aztec and Mayan civilizations encountered the Spaniard in Mexico, Europe gained sustenance like corn and tomatoes and began undying love affairs with chocolate and vanilla. In much the same way, the Inca encountered the Spaniard in Peru, and provided that same distant continent with the gold to become a powerful empire. Though most people today believe that tomatoes originated in Italy and potatoes in Ireland, these treasures from the rough earth were originally, in fact, precious exports from Mexico and Peru.

In what is now Brazil, European settlers speaking Portuguese encountered African slaves speaking a host of tribal languages. Over time, these slaves gave Brazil—especially its coastal state of Bahia that looks eastward to Africa—its own satisfying version of "soul food." The transfer of people, cultures, languages and foods that occurred during the golden age of exploration of the New World created what we consider to be regional cuisines today.

At the geographic center of these discoveries lay a long isthmus that became known as Central America. It forms the natural break from the vast distances, thick jungles and towering mountains separating Atlantic and Pacific oceans to the north and south. In the 19th century, brave souls began shaving weeks off their ocean-to-ocean journey by crossing the narrowest stretches of land by rail or carriage as they had earlier by foot. People and cargo were transported across Nicaragua so regularly that an industry developed. Other travelers preferred an even shorter crossing through nearby Panama, a practice that led to the creation of "the path between the seas," the Panama Canal, in 1914. That feat of engineering, and the Americans who wrought it, would change the Cordúa family story forever.

During Nicaragua's heyday as the ocean-to-ocean crossing point, American tycoon Cornelius Vanderbilt operated a railroad. Travelers came to Nicaragua as a means to reach somewhere else. For a variety of reasons, many chose to stay. This more contemporary melding of European and Latin cultures accounts for the large number of American and British surnames found among Nicaraguans, as well as for the close working relationships many of them had with American businesses. In this way, Melville Cordúa, Michael's grandfather, served in communications with Teddy Roosevelt on the American side of the Spanish-American War before joining the American company now known as AT&T and coming to the Canal Zone.

Before moving to the Canal Zone to manage the territory stretching from Mexico to Ecuador, Melville Cordúa married Anna Kelly, a young Irish woman from the Nicaraguan port town of San Juan del Sur. In 1923 Michael's father, Roberto, was born on what was defined by treaties as American soil. While he was still a child, Roberto's parents separated and he returned with his mother to Nicaragua. She would never leave the country again.

As Harry, Roberto's brother, was studying to be a priest, his mother came to view Roberto as the person who would support her. Roberto had to take whatever education he could get and go to work. Because he had been born in the Canal Zone, he was qualified to work at the U.S. Embassy in Managua, the country's capital. When he married Michael's mother, Dora, she was required to become a U.S. citizen because of his work. As a result, all seven of the couple's children had the right to choose American citizenship. The only passport Michael has ever carried is American.

"My Dad's work took him along several business paths, including into the shipping industry that would launch my career," says Michael. "Our family's position in the social world advanced. We lived in a large house in Managua with live-in help to tend the garden, do the laundry, iron, clean, cook and watch over the children." The help slept in quarters in the back of the house, but in Michael's mind, they were part of his family.

Since his parents did not prepare meals, Michael, with his love of food, felt closest to the cook. While many chefs'

When the Aztec and Mayan civilizations encountered the Spaniard in Mexico, Europe gained sustenance like corn and tomatoes and began undying love affairs with chocolate and vanilla.

stories include ventures into the kitchen at a tender age, in Nicaragua at that time, it would not have been considered appropriate for a child of the Patrón, much less a male child, to work in the kitchen. The cook made everything, whether it was *café con leche* at breakfast or one of the many beef dishes provided for dinner.

Like the other women she knew in Nicaragua, Michael's mother wrote the menu for the house each week and sent the kitchen help to the markets for all the local, tropical and Latin ingredients needed to prepare the recipes. She herself went to the American stores to pick up items from the States, mostly in cans of course, that were harder to get and therefore much more desirable. Michael remembers not so much the food she bought, but what it expressed. Her hospitality was one of abundance. His mother had fresh-squeezed orange juice to wake the family each morning, a hot morning snack, a hot homemade lunch, then an afternoon snack and finally a hot homemade dinner. It was all about loving her family. His father loved food, and his mother loved to make food for him. The Cordúa dynamic of hospitality was born in Dora Cordúa's open, hospitable home, where guests were always welcome. If there were no leftovers, she felt there hadn't been enough prepared.

Although there was always plenty of food, the farm-to-table life that many of us envision in traditional cultures was not an option. Sanitation was an issue, so everything the family ate was well-done to kill germs. Eventually this method of cooking became their taste preference as well. Michael's father ate beef, his mother chose lighter foods like fish, and he grew up without much exposure to vegetables or fruits. His appreciation of the nuances of these goods, like his love of seafood, came much later.

The foods Michael ate growing up form a litany of Latin tastes and are still favorites of his. Some are dishes enjoyed by different names in other Latin countries and some share the names of different dishes from other countries. Along with grilled beef and pork, he enjoyed *vigorón,* (yuca with fried pork rinds), *repochetas* (cheese-filled tortilla pockets that function as Nicaraguan grilled cheese sandwiches, *salpicón* (boiled beef ground and eaten with lime juice, green bell pepper, onion and rice) and *tamales,* both *yoltamal* and *nacatamal.* The first is essentially a vegan tamal made with fresh corn cut off the cob, rather than dried corn ground into masa. And the second is an extra-large tamal stuffed with pork, rice, onions, and a potpourri of spices cooked in a banana leaf.

More than any other food, the dish that defines childhood for Michael was *Gallo Pinto.* The name means Red Rooster, a reference to the small red kidney beans used in the recipe. Whatever else the Cordúas ate during the day, they usually enjoyed *Gallo Pinto* at all three meals, and a pot of the glorious stuff sat on the stove at all times.

When he was sixteen, Michael left Nicaragua for college in the States. He planned to return after he earned his degree, but revolution changed the course of his country and his life. He never returned to live in his homeland.

The overthrow of the Somoza dynasty in 1979 affected everyone in the Cordúas community. They went from living a life of relative luxury to having little money and fewer opportunities. Michael had entered Texas A&M as a banker-to-be, majoring in economics with a minor in finance, because he anticipated returning home to work with his uncles who were well established in Nicaraguan banking.

"I was a junior in college when the Sandinistas came to power," Michael says. "Had it happened sooner, I would not have gotten the opportunity to travel to College Station and become an Aggie."

During his years in College Station, without realizing it, Michael began taking steps that would eventually lead him to become a restaurateur, or a cook, as he prefers to call himself. He studied hard in class, worked hard at his student job as the cafeteria's warehouse manager and saw nice things that his life in Nicaragua had never shown him. Going out to eat with friends, he was drawn to all-you-can-eat buffets. Surrounded by a bounty of new, fresh foods, he tried everything, and his waistline expanded with his taste. He began to worry

> **More than any other food, the dish that defines childhood for Michael was *Gallo Pinto.***

> **Going out to eat with friends, he was drawn to all-you-can-eat buffets. Surrounded by a bounty of new, fresh foods, he tried everything.**

about the price of these meals compared to what he believed it would cost him to make the same food, or perhaps even better food, in his apartment. He taught himself how to fry ground beef and mastered the steaming of rice. The first time he tried to cook refried beans, a staple of his existence to date, he simply put the raw, dried beans in hot oil. The resulting dish resembled bad popcorn.

During his senior year at A&M, the general manager of the cafeteria where Michael worked was offered a job in shipping in Houston. The GM wasn't interested, because he wanted to go to Mexico and develop a chain of restaurants. He took Michael on a planning trip and gave him his first exposure to the restaurant business.

It was not yet time for Michael to embark on what was to become his life's work, however. Michael's former GM suggested that Michael go to Houston to interview for the shipping job. The revolution had destroyed his opportunities in Nicaraguan banking, and Michael believed the shipping training would enable him to return to work with his father. His father, however, had learned he was dying of cancer.

On December 26, 1980, Michael had borrowed $500 to marry Lucia Callejas. In 1982, David was born on July 1, and Michael's father's died on August 16. The loss of his father so closely following the birth of his son made Michael realize that what had begun as a training experience needed to become a permanent job.

As the world's petroleum hub, Houston had the heavy equipment needed for exploration and production. Whether oil was discovered as close as Venezuela or as far away as Kuwait or Abu Dhabi, the energy companies, and related services, needed equipment and supplies shipped to them. The company Michael worked for in Houston located equipment; identified ships to carry it; scheduled, booked and negotiated the cost; and guaranteed accurate, on-time delivery. Persevering through whatever situations developed—storms at sea, striking longshoremen in Naples or governments overthrown as his own had been at home—Michael rose through the company, eventually traveling the world as the owner's right-hand man.

"People always tell me: Oh, it must have been so much fun sailing to all those exotic ports," Michael says. "And I tell them: Look, no. I didn't sail much of anywhere. I was the guy who saw the ship off in Houston and two weeks later flew to the final destination to make sure it showed up. That was a great experience too, but not the romantic nautical adventure people always picture. When everything worked, which it usually did, there was excellent money to be made. Especially when the oil industry was booming."

Michael's five years in shipping transformed him. He would wear a good suit for meetings with shipping agents in London, then change into overalls to work beside longshoremen on the dock. As he got to know the dock-workers, he began frequenting their taquerias and late-night Greek belly-dancing bars. Once again, his palate was expanding with his world-view.

The company's owner also participated in Michael's food education. A former sea captain, he sought out the finest things from all over the world. His success allowed him the opportunity to enjoy them. Whether abroad or at home in Houston, he introduced Michael to dishes he never would have sampled on his own—sushi, for instance. Whatever reservations Michael might have had about trying raw fish on the beach in Nicaragua disappeared once he tasted the cool, clean flavors of the freshest fish.

Michael's travels took him frequently to London, Holland, Northern Germany and Scandinavia. His Spanish fluency made him the key figure in the company's Latin American deals, which increased as Mexico developed its oil industry. By the time the oil bust knocked Houston on its heels, he had been made a partner in the business and his understanding of food had been forever changed. When oil prices plummeted, however, the company's founder decided to retire and shut down the company. Michael needed to find a new direction.

He explored the possibility of exporting vegetables from Central America with his father-in-law, Alfonso Callejas, who had at one point exported vegetables grown in Nicaragua to sell in the Safeway chain of grocery stores. Alfonso knew the growers, and he knew the export-import policies, but he had lost everything in the revolution and did not have the capital to begin again. Michael and his father-in-law traveled all through Costa Rica, Honduras and

Guatemala, talking about deals with growers who might fit into their business plan. But unbeknownst to Michael, the CIA was also reaching out to his father-in-law and other members of his wife's family to work to destabilize the Sandinista government before it could carry nearby El Salvador along a similar path. They became part of the group known as the Contras. For Michael, these political circumstances meant that the vegetable business was not a possibility.

He considered buying a business, and explored the possibility of a high-end furniture retailer in Houston. Trade shows would have taken him abroad regularly, which appealed to him. Just as he was about to make the purchase, the store's current owner provided him with some important insight. "Michael, I'm not going to sell you my business," she said. "This is not what you're supposed to be doing."

The questioned remained: What was he supposed to do? What pursuit would support his family and engage his soul? He entered a period of intense introspection. As a Latin male, the code of *machismo* was very real to him. Just as there were certain things a man should always do, there were also those he should never do. Although the Nicaragua where he had grown up had disappeared, the constraints placed on males still lingered in his mind. One of the things he had always felt he wasn't allowed to be was a cook, and that was just what was calling to him.

Our Food, Our
LIFE

What ultimately helped Michael resolve his professional conflict was his personal life—his wife Lucia, their son David, and their daughters Michelle, Elisa and Cristina. The Cordúas' family life parallels and intertwines their restaurant life. Though he found his way to the restaurants through other experiences, Michael isn't sure if any of his children can remember him as anything but a cook.

He had known Lucia as far back as he could remember. Their fathers attended boarding school together in Nicaragua, and her brothers were Michael's friends growing up in Managua. Though her family moved out of the capital after the devastating earthquake of 1972, the families remained close. Because she was just his friends' little sister, Michael hadn't really noticed Lucia. Then, when she was nineteen, she transferred to A&M. In this new light, he saw her clearly. He proposed to her right after graduation in 1980, and they were married at St. Thomas More Church in Houston that December.

Before Lucia came to A&M, Michael had assumed he would marry an American. He had envisioned an attractive urban professional woman as his wife. They would have only one child, so they could focus on international travel and entertaining. But when Michael became reacquainted with the grown-up Lucia, he realized the YUPPY fantasy was not for him. He began his American professional life with a wife who, better than anyone, knew who he was and how his country had influenced him. Lucia left medical school to marry Michael, and together the Cordúas began building a home life that had food at its center.

As the family grew—with David's birth in 1982, Michelle's in June 1984, Elisa's in August 1987 and Cristina's in April 1989—Lucia also provided tremendous help to Michael at the first Churrascos restaurant. By the time she was pregnant with Cristina, she no longer had to come into the restaurant every day, but she still handled the payroll from home.

Although the restaurant business has notably long hours, it allowed Michael to do two things most 9-to-5 fathers never can: prepare breakfast and lunch for his family. Before school Michael made them whatever they felt like eating, which meant Nicaraguan standards like *Gallo Pinto* as well as eggs, bacon, sausage, pancakes and waffles. But he also found himself cooking more daringly, sometimes to their visible displeasure. After Michael served them a morning meal of spaghetti carbonara, young David spoke up for the group in protest: "Dad, don't experiment with us at breakfast!"

Michael often sent his children to school with triple-decker sandwiches, high-quality cold cuts plus honey mustard or intriguing touches like maple syrup. The word got out, and before long David was selling his lunches to other students.

Then, when he was only forty-six, Michael was diagnosed with a pulmonary embolism. He remembers his brother Glenn visiting him in the hospital and asking if he was afraid to die. "I told him no," Michael says. "All I really felt was gratitude. That's the price of a good death, I believe—a good life." Michael emerged with a deep reverence for every day he was alive. He reassessed the way he was living—his weight, his food and drink, his lifestyle.

As he began a long recovery, Michael was invited to participate in something called the American Leadership Forum, which provided an unexpected encounter not only with other people's ideas about business but also with new ideas about life and even the spirituality at the heart of it all. With this broadened perspective, Michael began work on his MBA. He graduated with the desire to grow the restaurant business he had begun with the first Churrascos.

Michael's past had taught him that there were as many nuances to Latin food as there were countries and communities. The Nicaraguan cuisine of his childhood shared few flavors with Mexican food, and fewer with the popular Tex-Mex. In his travels abroad, he had experienced the traditional dishes of Spain and other Latin American countries. And in the states, he'd been to other American cities like Miami, and eaten with the Cubans along Calle Ocho who had their own traditions. He knew the range of Latin flavors and dishes, but he wondered if anyone in Texas, a place so enamored with its interpretation of Mexican food, would let a Nicaraguan into the kitchen.

From the moment in 1987 that Michael started planning the first Churrascos, he didn't think of it as "Nicaraguan." His many friends and acquaintances who loved the Nicaraguan dishes he cooked for them at home assumed these traditional foods would be the menu. Michael saw an all-Nicaraguan restaurant as limiting. He told them, "There are five-thousand Nicaraguans in the greater Houston area, but there are five-million people." His desire to share the foods of his homeland was broad, encompassing his entire Latin heritage and the large community of the city he now called home. A small, nostalgic menu that would appeal to a limited audience did not leave room for his experience of what food could be.

He began looking for a location for his new restaurant, but everywhere he looked

> **"I very much had in mind the style of beef cookery I remembered from Nicaragua, which had been imported from the cattle-crazed pampas of Argentina."**

inside Houston's I-610 Loop, the brokers demanded restaurant experience in addition to a downpayment. He was denied an entry for eleven miles. He began his search in the bohemian neighborhood known as Montrose, and he continued to be told no all the way out to what would become Beltway 8. The space he leased eventually had already seen eight restaurants fail. It had the look of a ship, even though Michael was trying to open a steakhouse. The neighborhood was on its way down rather than up, but the Cordúas finally had a location. What the place needed now was a name.

Describing his initial plans, Michael recalls, "I very much had in mind the style of beef cookery I remembered from Nicaragua, which had been imported from the cattle-crazed pampas of Argentina. Over the years, since the traditional skirt steaks back home were too tough, Nicaraguans had started using tenderloin and cutting it in a way that resembled skirt steak. The notion of making more expensive beef resemble less expensive beef may strike you as odd, but it wouldn't after you tasted the churrasco served in Nicaragua."

The first few times Michael prepared beef this way for his friends in Houston, they thought he was making a type of fajita. Though they complimented the food, he was disheartened, and he made the very costly decision to replace the beef with American corn fed premium aged beef as the team worked toward opening. The restaurant would be Churrascos.

Michael was proud of his opening day menu, from the namesake churrasco to the fresh and flavorful seafood to the lush, homestyle desserts. The Cordúas were on their way in the restaurant business. But how well he remembers: "The first few tables we seated on opening night did the one thing I'd never factored into any of my plans. They looked at the menu and, with varying degrees of politeness, stood up and walked out. What they wanted, you see, was Tex-Mex. And that was the very thing we couldn't and wouldn't give them."

In opening Churrascos, the Cordúas created a unique restaurant category. But as others who've created categories will attest, that meant there was nobody to buy the product right away. The first months were more difficult than he could have imagined, and to keep things running, Michael had to use the family's savings to cover both payroll and rent. Just as he said to himself, "Oh my God, we're going to close down," diners began to understand what he was trying to do. That January was the first month the restaurant was able to cover its own expenses. And two months after that, the wife of a Houston banker came in to talk to him about opening Churrascos No.2.

Without realizing it, the Cordúas were part of something that was just dawning on the national food scene. There weren't many people doing it yet. The movement, which some called Nuevo Latino, embraced and promoted many of the beliefs and techniques that Michael was struggling to introduce on the outskirts of Houston. Rather

than presenting dishes as Nicaraguan—or Peruvian or Chilean or Colombian—he presented them simply as Latin. Even more importantly, Michael didn't research and replicate traditional recipes; he created entirely new dishes from traditional foods and flavors, sometimes combining delicious elements of several classics from more than a single Latin country.

Years later, Houston-based author and restaurant critic Robb Walsh gave his summary of what Michael had achieved: "This culinary pioneer showed us the flavors, aromas and dishes of lands such as Nicaragua, Peru, Chile, Argentina and Brazil, expanding our vocabulary with words

like plantains, ceviches, empanadas, yuca, chimichurri and, of course, tres leches. The trail he blazed has inspired many other Latin cuisine concepts, broadening our culinary horizons far beyond Mexico."

When people say that restaurants are a "people business," they mean "dealing with customers." But as Michael quickly discovered, restaurants are a people business behind the scenes, too. Just as the shipping industry had broadened his palate, it also allowed him to move freely between wealthy executives in London and longshoremen on the dock. Understanding the value of each type of work, and being able to relate comfortably with people from all backgrounds proved to be the basis for his restaurant life.

Early on, he heard about and then met a young chef from Mexico named Gumaro Lopez. Gumaro, naturally, knew the Mexican food he'd grown up eating, but his mastery of classic French technique had landed him a chef's job at Houston's famous La Tour d'Argent. Mentors are usually older than their pupils, but the younger Gumaro became Michael's mentor in the kitchen.

Gumaro and his fellow professionals (including Tere Ocampo, known as the "Julia Child of Peru," who made the restaurant's first desserts) were able to teach Michael what he needed to know about making serious food. This type of lesson, now taught by the Culinary Institute of America and other professional training centers, had for centuries been passed down from master to apprentice. These chefs were able to create dishes based on the wisdom of French technique but also capturing the ingredients of authentic Latin cooking. And, in ways that would prove invaluable as the Cordúas opened restaurants with different concepts, they were able to ground him in how a true "production kitchen" works, keeping the quality and consistency at its highest even when the quantities were enormous.

In his school days in Nicaragua, the Jesuits had taught Michael he wasn't creative. During his years in shipping, he believed they'd been right.

"As the saying goes, I had a sharp pencil," Michael says. "And in logistics, it was my job to deliver the product on time at the right cost. In the restaurant business, I discovered a life that didn't simply allow me to be creative—it pretty much *demanded* it. From the look and feel of the restaurant to the menu, from the recipes to their consistent execution, from the biggest bigwig in the dining room to the lowliest

dishwasher at the back of the kitchen, I had to be creative every day I went to work. I loved it. And I especially loved knowing that, for all their insights about so many things, the Jesuits had been totally wrong about me."

Less than two years after opening Churrascos eleven miles west of where Michael had wanted to be, the Cordúas opened the second Churrascos on Shepherd near Westheimer—a true crossroads of Houston's social and business life. That location remains wildly popular to this day, drawing not only from that neighborhood around Montrose but from River Oaks and Tanglewood as well. No one was likely to mistake the restaurant for a Tex-Mex taqueria ever again. Now that Churrascos had found its audience, ran smoothly and regularly delighted diners, the Cordúas began envisioning a new concept.

A location had opened up near the Galleria mall on Post Oak. Houston icons Robert del Grande and Tony Vallone had restaurants within a few steps: Café Annie (which would morph into RDG) and Tony's. Both had generational followings, as well as years of national and international media. If the family went into this location, they'd have to enter in a manner that could share the spotlight with these talented chefs and their lauded restaurants.

The space, on the back of a retail development, was large, open and imposing. Michael had a Nicaraguan architect working on design ideas, until he had to move back to Nicaragua in the middle of the design. Michael was without an architect when he met a creative young man named Jordan Mozer. In his designs for a restaurant called The Tempest, Mozer was evoking the magical elements of Shakespeare's play about people shipwrecked on an island where nothing is what it seems. Michael saw Jordan's work, and he understood. He began talking to Jordan about this new restaurant, which had taken on the ambitious name Américas.

"The Americas, I told him, aren't exactly a melting pot," explains Michael. "Groups of people didn't come here and disappear. They came here with their culture,

or maybe they started out here with their culture, and it changed but it never went away. No, the Americas were more of a basket weave, drawing elements from all over the world that had never existed in the same place before, and weaving them together to create something new. That something was colorful, that something was glistening, and that something was adventurous, calling out to all who shared the same sense of adventure."

Jordan created an abstract rendition of the Amazon rainforest in the style of Gaudí and Picasso. Guests entered across a kind of bridge, metaphorically leaving all that was familiar behind. Together, Jordan and the Cordúas created a shimmering new world of glass and tile, ready to welcome a new cuisine born in a new world.

For Michael as a cook and for the family's restaurant business, Américas was both the next step and the next level. It did what they'd done since the first Churrascos: making food that evoked a large, diverse Latin mythology. And it did this in a fine-dining setting that balanced elegance with fun. Américas surprised and delighted diners and reviewers, being named a Best New Restaurant in America by *Esquire* and earning Michael one of the coveted spots as *Food & Wine's* Best New Chefs. America was embracing food, wine and their purveyors as major news, and it was celebrating Michael's vision.

In addition to being his family's name, *Cordúa* had become a brand, and the family had to define it. Looking at what they had accomplished, they saw several key elements. They were Latin, they were innovative and they saw themselves as leaders in an industry that mostly has followers. They cared unceasingly about service, whatever the atmosphere or the price point. And, most of all, they served only food that was *yummy*. Michael's only unflinching position became: *First, make it yummy.*

Since then, the Cordúas have taken the values of their brand into many arenas. They entered the crowded fast-casual restaurant segment when they opened the first Amazón Grill in 1999. The introduction of Latin flavors into this market proved successful, and Michael plans for Amazón Grill eventually to expand to numerous locations. Broadening their culinary brushstroke to take in French, Italian and Asian flavors, the family opened Artista within Houston's downtown Hobby Center for the Performing Arts. Additionally, they have continued to expand their catering division, allowing fans to enjoy favorite Cordúa dishes in their homes and other venues.

As the 21ˢᵗ century drew near, the Américas restaurant that had been so monumental to the Cordúas demanded attention. For several years, the family had been watching developments in The Woodlands, an upscale community about thirty miles north of Houston. Though George Mitchell, the founder, had a vision that included a city center, the area had remained a bedroom community for people who worked in Houston. As satellite offices and telecommuting increased, people in The Woodlands were tending to work and play near their homes. The Cordúas believed it was time to expand northward with a new Américas.

"We wanted something different," says Michael. "Yes, we could have replicated the original and just opened the doors, but we were thinking otherwise. For one thing, it was a different audience. Then it was a different physical layout, sloping down to a waterway. And finally, Américas in The Woodlands was the first restaurant we created after David joined the company. His ideas were joining my ideas, and the result was, and always is, something different."

The family worked with Ilan Waisbrod and Yuni Rosita of New York-based Estudio Gaia on the project. Michael and David shared the basic Américas narrative, as Michael had with Jordan Mozer on Post Oak years before, and gave them license to create. Rather than a glistening rainforest of glass, the second Américas emerged as a temple within that rainforest.

Like ancient gods and goddesses, diners descend glowing golden steps entering the temple to be served bowls of Aztec and Maya offerings like cacao, maize, vanilla and tropical flowers. Large photographic panels on the ceiling present scenes from the rainforest. The patio along the waterway evokes the bow of a ship, with awnings of cream-colored fabric billowing out like sails. All the elements combine to suggest that the voyage continues: the Americas are still being discovered.

As the Cordúas were getting their Woodlands operation in order, they were forced to reasses the original Américas. The developers planned to tear down the whole complex to make room for a new generation of restaurants. The Cordúas would have to start over. But, when it came to where and how, the slate was blank. Plans for the next Américas quickly came together around a space at the edge of Houston's most renowned neighborhood. Américas River Oaks was born.

Once again, the Cordúas chose to work with Jordan Mozer to design the space.

"If you got married and had Christian Dior design your wedding dress," Michael said shortly after opening, "and then you got married again twenty years later, you wouldn't expect Dior to create the same dress, now would you? That first Américas was the work of very young men, myself included, all excitement and adventure, like Indiana Jones. Now we're quieter and more thoughtful about how and why we make magic."

In addition to being his family's name, *Cordúa* had become a brand, and the family had to define it.

The décor borrows from the Columbus-era New World without literally representing any part of it. There are, for instance, two wall installations known to the staff as "homage to squash" and "homage to beans," both evoking crucial food products of the Americas in a playful way. David, trained at Le Cordon Bleu in Paris, has joined Michael in the kitchen, representing the future of this restaurant family. Father counts on son not simply to be an excellent cook, but also to see into the future in ways he cannot, to know what *his* generation will want from Cordúa restaurants; and, if they succeed, what David's children's generation will want.

"I wouldn't have the vision I have today without David to share and expand upon it," says Michael. "David also reminds me that our lives are not merely days but the *stories* of days. And these stories are the precious gifts we give to all who come after us."

Homeward
BOUND

Food was part of David Cordúa's life as far back as he can remember.

By the time he started paying attention, his father had turned his experiences into the first Churrascos. David was only six when the restaurant opened, but he remembers friends and family plus other members of Houston's Nicaraguan community coming to dinner parties at the house to taste the recipes as they evolved.

"I **might have thought we** were opening a Nicaraguan restaurant, since so many of the people who came over were displaced Nicaraguans in the aftermath of the revolution down there," David recalls. "Now, of course, I understand that my father had no such thing in mind. He was a part—a leader, in fact— of another revolution that would carry a broader vision of Latin cuisine into the heart of Texas."

He remembers visiting Churrascos, and the dank smell of a building that had earlier stored, cooked and served seafood. Michael was in the kitchen in those early days, along with a chef and some line cooks he'd managed to hire from other Houston restaurants. His mother, Lucia, was the hostess and his uncle and aunt were daily parts of the operation, too.

After school, David would come to the restaurant. It was a great place for an after-school snack. He ate *pollo en salsa blanca* or a sandwich called a *pepito*: slices of wonderful beef churrasco served between two pieces of garlic bread. David ate very little peanut butter and jelly in his childhood, which probably explains why he loves that combination so much today.

Before he was ten, David started fixing little meals for his parents and eventually for his sisters. One of his less successful efforts was his version of British "toad in the hole." Instead of cutting a hole in toast to soft-cook the egg, David used a tortilla. A more pleasing creation was his fried chicken—each piece marinated first in bottled Italian dressing, and definitely qualifying as yummy.

Michael and Lucia Cordúa and most of their first friends were Latin. Yet David was growing up in America. His classmates did not share or, for the most part, understand his Nicaraguan roots. He felt he needed to fling his arms around all things American, especially in terms of culture, which to him meant *pop* culture. Fitting in is important to every young person's development, but to David, fitting in meant being American.

He loved American movies. For David, they mattered more than simple entertainment. He loved Spielberg and Lucas, and he knew everything about Star Wars. He particularly loved the way the ideas, the stories and especially the characters in all these iconic films taught him how to be American. In seventh grade, he convinced his English teacher to let the class make a film. He was the director.

He also loved music, especially the styles he considered most American—jazz, classic rock, blues and funk. Through high school at Strake Jesuit in Houston, he played in a band called The Newspaper Taxis, a reference to "Lucy in the Sky with Diamonds" from the Beatles' *Sgt. Pepper* album.

After Strake, he enrolled in Santa Clara University, where his grandfather had been a member of the Class of 1948. He loved the school from the first time he saw it, when his grandfather took him to his 50th reunion. David, on the advice of his father, majored in business. Silicon Valley was an exciting place to be at the peak of the dot.com boom.

"There was such a can-do feeling in the valley, with graduates walking off the stage with diplomas into high-salary positions at one of the software companies right up the street," David remembers. "There were new products in the air every day, fresh ideas, huge investments. Like I say, it was great to see that all in action. But even as a finance major, I knew I wanted something more. And in bits and pieces during college, I started trying to track it down."

Having grown up hearing what his father learned traveling the world, David felt it would be important for him to venture abroad, too. In his junior year he traveled as a student to Cuba for three months, then took his sister Michelle backpacking through Thailand, tasting exotic dishes for almost no money. Finally, he signed up for a semester in London, via a Syracuse University program. He was so broke in London that he couldn't experience the restaurants. He remembers cooking for himself every day at home, even while taking a class called "Food, Culture and Identity."

Returning to Santa Clara to graduate, he watched as his finance-major friends applied for jobs, mostly with large accounting firms and investment banks. David applied for (and got) a job as a breakfast cook in a local hotel.

It was a very nice hotel, run by the Valencia Group. It allowed David to work with a talented chef named Mercer Mohr, who coincidentally had been famous back in Houston at the Omni. After Mohr left

> Michael and Lucia Cordúa and most of their first friends were Latin. Yet David was growing up in America. His classmates did not share, or for the most part, understand his Nicaraguan roots.

Silicon Valley, David found his way into other kitchen jobs, including one with Randy Lewis, former executive chef at Kendall-Jackson, at a restaurant called Popina in Sonoma's wine country. This was the first place he saw what would later be the norm: dressed-down fine dining, with waiters wearing T-shirts serving hyper-fresh, hyper-local ingredients. At this point, David knew culinary school was in his future. Where to go and what to study remained questions.

"I could go to Spain, where so much of traditional cuisine was being turned on its ear by Ferran Adria's molecular cuisine at El Bulli," he recalls. "Or I could go to sushi school in Los Angeles, since I'd known my once-carnivore Dad only after he'd fallen in love with sushi. Or I could go to Le Cordon Bleu in Paris, hoping to master the very same food traditions that Adria and his followers were shaking up. Considering the things I saw my Dad doing, the way he approached foods of the Americas by way of French technique, my choice eventually became as obvious as it somehow hadn't been for so long."

David spent two years in the French capital at Le Cordon Bleu, and then another year cooking in Parisian commercial kitchens. He lived in a tumbledown apartment in the Latin Quarter close to Place Saint-Michel. His building was so old that the floor slanted at about a sixty-degree angle. He had a sink, a bed and a chair. He bought a 1970s brown Schwinn bicycle for getting to school and touring around. It was, he insists, the best time of his life.

The studies at Le Cordon Bleu, lasting twelve to fourteen hours six days a week, engaged and challenged him. There was nothing academic, bookish or philosophical, simply demonstration and practice, over and over until each aspect of a dish was mastered. In the early part of the program an English translator was present, but every lesson afterward was conducted in French.

David and his best friend, a young man from Greece, had made a pact to jump off the Pont Saint-Michel into the Seine wearing their chef's whites on the last day of the program. They did this on a Saturday afternoon, with tourists from all over the world looking on. The two graduates barely made it to the bank before the *bateau de police* took them into custody. Happily, the officers let them off with a stern warning.

After completing Le Cordon Bleu in 2005, part of David wanted to head straight home and take his place in the Cordúa restaurant company. But he wanted to do something more too, and that took another full year. *Stages,* the French word pronounced *STAH-jes,* are short stints in kitchen after kitchen, a terrific way for chefs-in-the-making to increase and diversify their skill sets. Sensing the life he had ahead of him, David decided to stay in France.

He learned some good things at the Paris classic La Tour d'Argent, where (in the time-honored French tradition) he was mostly a "peon wearing a funny hat." He learned even more working at L'Auberge Bressane, a place devoted to the cooking of northwest France around Normandy, rich with cream and butter, terrines and pâtés. He spent time in an Italian pizzeria/enoteca, continuing the wine education he'd begun in northern California.

When David eventually moved back from Paris, he returned to California rather than Texas, taking a job as food and beverage manager of a 150-room hotel with two restaurants, a conference center and a wedding venue. In addition to creating highly personalized menus for each event he put together, David focused on wine pairing and began experimenting as a mixologist. Now, his knowledge of a good bar ensures that Cordúa restaurants serve top-shelf cocktails, many with nods to the Americas, and David has hands-on involvement in their creation.

When his father invited him to New York to meet with the architect for the new Américas in The Woodlands, David realized it was time to return home.

"Getting that Américas to opening day was an awesome time for me, to learn and to grow," David remembers. "We actually put together a Peruvian food festival at Artista in preparation, inviting five super chefs from Peru to come and create menus for night after night of sold-out dinners. I'm confident no one in Artista's dining room learned as much from these guys as I did. And having come into the company the way I did, with so much collaboration at the heart of my journey, I also wanted to see what other Houston chefs could bring to our project. We brought in a series of highly creative guys, some a better fit for

us than others. My father stood back and let me do what I believed we needed, and for that I'm grateful."

Not every creative touch David tried at the new Américas worked out, and the global recession began changing the landscape. David learned how to incorporate the Cordúa traditions the customers loved, in a new look and a new location. By the time the family closed the original Américas and opened Américas River Oaks, David had clarified his thinking—primarily by working to launch the catering department. This experience, plus creating the menus Michael and David would offer at the new Américas, gave this father and son chef team the most comprehensive understanding they'd ever had of the balance between tradition and innovation.

Mapping out their future, David and his family use this understanding as their compass. Combining the foods and flavors of their homeland with the techniques they have learned on their travels, the Cordúas' adventure in food continues to venture into new territory. Whether it is traditional, revolutionary or a combination of the two, every dish they serve in the future will bear the Cordúa signature—it will be delightful, it will be beautiful and it will be yummy.

"My father stood back and let me do what I believed we needed, and for that I'm grateful."

Perfect
BITES

A French chef might call these small tasting portions *hors d'oeuvres;* but more and more in our kitchens, we refer to them as perfect bites. We do that for a couple of reasons. For one thing, they are the way we like to eat, whether we're cooking at home or in a restaurant. We'd rather have one bite of thirty things than thirty bites of one thing. We also respond well to a challenge. A single bite, passed or set out at a wedding or event, has to balance acid and fat, sweet and sour. It has to deliver the excitement of discovery and the comfort of familiar, and it has to do it fast. It's a symphony of flavor that must say a lot with a little.

PLANTAIN CHIPS AND SAUCES

ROASTED TOMATO SAUCE

4 guajillo peppers

12 chile de arbol

12 cloves garlic

10 Roma tomatoes

3 jalapenos

1 tablespoon salt

1 tablespoon sugar

HUANCAINA SAUCE

5 tablespoons aji amarillo paste

1 tablespoon chopped onion, marinated at least 1 day in malt vinegar

1 ½ cup crumbled queso fresco

¾ cup cotija cheese

¼ cup crushed Saltine cracker

1 teaspoon salt

1 ¼ cup evaporated milk

1 cup corn oil

CILANTRO SAUCE

1 bunch cilantro

4 cloves garlic

½ jalapeno

¼ cup white wine vinegar

½ cup water

1 teaspoon salt

2 cups mayonnaise

PLANTAIN CHIPS

5 green plantains

Vegetable oil to deep fry

Salt

IF THERE'S ANY SINGLE THING THAT LETS YOU KNOW YOU'RE IN ONE OF OUR RESTAU-RANTS, IT'S THE HAPPY PRESENCE OF PLANTAIN CHIPS. IN NICARAGUA THEY ARE A STREET FOOD KNOWN AS "TAJADAS" OR STRIPS. IN OTHER LATIN COUNTRIES THEY ARE A COMMON MOVIE THEATER SNACK. THE COLORS OF THE DIPPING SAUCES INSPIRE US TO CALL THEM THE STOPLIGHT. THERE'S HUANCAINA FROM PERU, MEXICAN-INSPIRED ROASTED TOMATO AND OUR CREAMY CILANTRO SAUCE.

Roasted Tomato Sauce: Preheat oven to 375° F. Remove the stems from the guajillo and chile de arbol peppers, and roast them with the garlic in a dry pan until lightly charred. On a hot grill, char the tomatoes and jalapenos until blistered. Combine with the dry peppers and garlic on a roasting pan and set in the oven for 15 minutes. Using a blender or food processor, purée the mixture until smooth and add the salt and sugar. Makes about 1 quart.

Huancaina Sauce: Place all the ingredients except oil in a food processor and purée until smooth. Then, as though making mayonnaise, set the processor on high speed and gradually pour in the oil, letting each addition incorporate fully. Makes about 1 quart.

Cilantro Sauce: Place all ingredients except the mayonnaise in a food processor and purée until a green liquid results. Spoon the mayonnaise into a large mixing bowl and fold the purée into it. Makes about 1 quart.

Plantain Chips: Preheat the oil in a pan or fryer to 350° F. Thinly slice in plantains lengthwise using a mandolin or other slicer. Fry until golden, 2-3 minutes. Drain and salt to taste. Serves 8.

CEVICHE COPACABANA

POACHED SHRIMP

½ yellow onion, chopped

3 cloves garlic

1 lemon, cut in half

3 bay leaves

1 gallon water

1 teaspoon salt

½ pound shrimp, shell on

LECHE DE TIGRE

1 cup lime juice

½ cup shrimp poaching liquid

½ cup brine from canned jalapenos

4 cloves garlic

¼ onion

1 pound tilapia, cut into ¼ by 2 inch slices

Julienned red onion

Julienned jalapeno

Chopped cilantro

WITH THE HEAT ALONG THE GULF COAST, THESE COOLING, FLAVORFUL VARIATIONS ON CEVICHE ARE PARTICULAR DELIGHTS. LONG ASSOCIATED WITH THE BEACHES OF MEXICO, EVEN MORE REVERED VARIETIES NOW COME FROM THE COAST OF PERU. AT CHURRASCOS, SEAFOOD CEVICHE QUICKLY BECAME THE PERFECT APPETIZER BEFORE OUR GUESTS DUG INTO A STEAK. WE MAKE THIS CEVICHE WITH PERUVIAN *LECHE DE TIGRE*—TIGER'S MILK—AND WE ADD A BIT OF FISH BROTH TO MELLOW OUT THE BITE OF THE LIME JUICE.

To poach shrimp, bring all ingredients except shrimp to a boil and let simmer a few minutes for flavors to meld. Add shrimp and poach just until pink. Remove from heat and let cool. When cool, peel the shrimp and return both shrimp and shells to the poaching liquid. Let sit in refrigerator for at least an hour.

Make the *Leche de Tigre* by combining all ingredients in a blender and puréeing. In a bowl, combine the tilapia with the *Leche de Tigre* and let sit for about 45 minutes. To serve, remove poached shrimp from liquid with shells and combine with fish. Mix in red onion, jalapeno and cilantro and serve in a hollowed-out pineapple shell. Serves 2.

TUNA CEVICHE

LIME DASHI JUICE

2 cups fresh lime juice

1 ¾ cups chopped onion

¼ cup chopped carrot

¼ cup chopped celery

2 whole peeled garlic cloves

3 tablespoons chopped jalapeno

1 teaspoon chopped ginger root

1 tablespoon kosher salt

2 cups fish stock
(1 ½ teaspoons dry hon dashi
dissolved in 2 cups hot water)

¼ cup sugar

4 tablespoons ponzu citrus
soy sauce

½ tablespoon sesame oil

1 pound fresh tuna, sliced
and pounded out paper-thin

¼ cup tablespoons julienned
jicama

4 tablespoons diced red onion

4 tablespoons chopped cilantro

2 teaspoons kosher salt

¼ cup crushed honey roasted
peanuts

¼ cup prepared hoisin sauce

SINCE MANY OF OUR GUESTS FOUND THEIR COMFORT LEVEL WITH CEVICHE BY LEARN-ING TO LOVE SUSHI, WE THINK IT'S THE MOST NATURAL THING IN THE WORLD TO IN-CORPORATE ASIAN FLAVORS INTO THIS TRADITIONAL LATIN PREPARATION WITH JAPA-NESE *HON DASHI* ALONG WITH CHINESE HOISIN SAUCE AND FRIED ONION.

Combine all Lime Dashi Juice ingredients in a container with a lid. Whisk briefly to dissolve. Let marinate in the refrigerator for 24 hours. Strain out vegetables and discard.

To make the final ceviche marinade, combine the ponzu sauce with the soy and 1 cup of the Lime Dashi Juice. Spread the paper-thin tuna on 4 plates and spoon the combined sauce over the top. Form a mound of jicama in the center of each, then sprinkle around the edges with red onion, cilantro, salt and roasted peanuts. Dot the fish with hoisin sauce. Serves 4.

SALMON CEVICHE

1 cup Lime Dashi Juice

4 tablespoons ponzu citrus soy sauce

½ tablespoon sesame oil

¼ pound smoked salmon, julienned

1 tablespoon toasted sesame seeds

1 pound salmon, sliced and pounded out paper-thin

2 tablespoons diced red onion

2 tablespoons diced jalapeno

1 tablespoon diced pineapple

1 tablespoon chopped cilantro

½ teaspoon kosher salt

1 teaspoon diced red bell pepper

PEOPLE DON'T USUALLY THINK OF SALMON WHEN THEY THINK OF CEVICHE—AND WE THINK THAT'S A SHAME. OURS SHOWS UP PREPARED TWO DIFFERENT WAYS: ONE IS A LIGHTLY ASIANIZED CEVICHE, THE OTHER SMOKED AND ROLLED UP WITH A MIX OF JALAPENO AND PINEAPPLE PROVING SWEET HEAT. TOASTED SESAME ALSO ENHANCES THE SMOKE FLAVOR.

In a bowl, combine the Lime Dashi Juice with the ponzu and sesame oil to make the Ceviche Marinade. Roll the julienned smoked salmon in the sesame seeds, pressing gently to coat. Position the thinly sliced salmon on 4 large plates and ladle citrus marinade over the top. Sprinkle the red onion, jalapeno and pineapple over the top of the fish. Sprinkle with chopped cilantro and salt. Arrange the sesame-coated smoked salmon around the plate and garnish with red bell pepper. Serves 4.

SPINACH RICOTTA GNUDI

BORN AT ARTISTA, *DESNUDAS* IS THE SPANISH NAME FOR ITALIAN *GNUDI,* MEANING NAKED. WHAT'S "NAKED" ABOUT THESE DELIGHTFUL BITES IS THAT THEY ARE ESSENTIALLY RAVIOLI WITHOUT ANY PASTA. THIS TERRIFIC SPINACH-RICOTTA FILLING IS BOUND TOGETHER BY FLOUR AND EGG, POACHED LIKE A DUMPLING AND THEN SAUTÉED WITH A LUSH SAUCE OF PORCINI AND CREAM.

Using a kitchen towel, squeeze all the water from the spinach. When spinach has cooled to room temperature, combine in a food processor with all remaining ingredients. Working with floured hands on a clean, floured surface, divide the dough into 1 tablespoon sized balls and quickly roll like small meatballs. Cook in boiled salted water as though they were gnocchi, removing them as soon as they float. Toss with Poricini Cream Sauce and serve immediately. Makes about 60 desnudas.

PORCINI CREAM SAUCE

Bring the water to a boil in a pan and then pour it over the dried porcini in a bowl, letting the mushrooms steep for 15 minutes. Meanwhile, sauté the onions in the butter just until they turn translucent. Add the rehydrated porcini and any remaining water to the pan, followed by the milk, cream and concentrated chicken stock and bay leaf. Let simmer 5 minutes. Remove bay leaf and stir in the cheese.

1 cup blanched spinach

1 egg

½ cup whole milk ricotta

½ cup finely grated Parmesan

2 ½ tablespoons all-purpose flour

PORCINI CREAM SAUCE

1 cup water

1 ounce dried porcini mushrooms

¼ cup diced onion

¼ cup butter

2 ½ cups whole milk

1 ⅓ cup heavy cream

2 tablespoons chicken stock, concentrated (see recipe p. 202)

1 bay leaf

⅓ cup Parmesan cheese

MARINEROS

MY FATHER FIRST CREATED THIS SIGNATURE FINGER FOOD AS HE REMEMBERED THE AROMA OF BURNING CORNFIELDS BACK HOME IN NICARAGUA, SOMETHING THAT WAS DONE AFTER THE HARVEST EACH YEAR TO ADD NUTRIENTS TO THE SOIL FOR THE NEXT PLANTING. WE TRIED SEVERAL VERSIONS OF CORN—FROM THE COBS TO EVERYDAY CORN TORTILLAS—BUT THEY ALL TURNED OUT TOO BITTER, UNTIL WE HIT ON USING THE HUSKS. THIS WAY THE CRAB FINGERS FROM THE NEARBY GULF OF MEXICO GET A SUBTLE, LIGHTLY SWEET TASTE, WHICH BENEFITS ROYALLY FROM THE CLASSIC FRENCH SAUCE OF BUTTER AND LEMON TOUCHED WITH DEMI-GLACE.

Prepare the Lemon Butter Sauce by combining the demi-glace the lemon and lime juices over medium heat until syrupy. Whisk in the butter a spoonful at a time until incorporated, being careful to lower heat and not let it boil. Taste and add salt. Keep warm.

Place the husks in a stove-top smoker and cover with a perforated pan or grill. Spread the crab fingers onto the pan or cover with lid or aluminum foil. Set smoker over burner on high heat and let smoke for 3 minutes, turn off heat and smoke 2 minutes more. When ready to serve, heat the olive oil in a pan and sauté the onion, green onion, bell pepper and jalapeno. Add the crab fingers and cook until lightly browned.

Deglaze the pan by adding the white wine and water. Ladle the sauce into the pan and swirl it around the crab fingers, letting it pick up the smoky taste. Transfer the crab fingers to a platter and generously spoon sauce over the top. Garnish with additional diced vegetables, if desired. Serves 8.

LEMON BUTTER SAUCE

1 teaspoon beef stock, concentrated

2 tablespoons lemon juice

2 tablespoons lime juice

2 sticks unsalted butter, softened at room temperature

1 teaspoon salt

6 corn husks

1 ½ pounds blue crab fingers

1 tablespoon olive oil

1 teaspoon diced onion

1 teaspoon diced green onion

1 teaspoon diced red bell pepper

1 teaspoon diced jalapeno

1 tablespoon white wine

1 tablespoon water

CORN AND CRAB TAMALES

12 corn husks

2 cups fresh or frozen corn kernels

1 tablespoon water

1 cup cornstarch

2 tablespoons sugar

1 teaspoon salt

1 teaspoon baking powder

1 cup melted butter

1 ½ pound lump crabmeat

Thinly sliced tarragon

Addition crabmeat

Habanero Beurre Blanc (see recipe p. 128)

THE MAKING OF TAMALES IS ONE OF THE MOST FUNDAMENTAL COOKING TECHNIQUES OF THE AMERICAS, A PLACE WHERE GROWING, HARVESTING AND GRINDING CORN HAS ALWAYS BEEN A MATTER OF SURVIVAL, EVOLVED INTO A MATTER OF ENJOYMENT, THE *MASA HARINA* IS REPLACED HERE WITH FRESH CORN PUREE AND MARRIES WELL WITH THE SWEETNESS OF FRESH CRABMEAT. YOU CAN STEAM THEM WITH ANY POT AND ANY TRAY OR PAN THAT HAS HOLES FOR STEAM. THE POPULAR ASIAN BAMBOO STEAMERS WORK WELL, TOO.

Soak the corn husks in water for 20-30 minutes to make them more pliable. Meanwhile, purée the corn kernels with 1 tablespoon water until smooth, then strain through a sieve into a bowl, to remove any tough pieces. In a large mixing bowl, combine the cornstarch with the sugar, salt and baking powder. Pour the puréed corn into these dry ingredients, followed by the melted butter, whisking together to form a batter.

Gently fold in the crabmeat, being careful not to crush the delicate meat. Using a spoon, fill the corn husks with the corn-crabmeat batter, about 1 ½ tablespoons per husk. Seal by folding under at one end. Set them on a steamer pan. Seal the pan with aluminum foil and set over boiling water to steam for 30 minutes. When ready, remove the husks and set tamales on platter or plate. Garnish with sliced tarragon, extra lump crabmeat and Habanero Beurre Blanc. Makes about 12 tamales.

CORN

If you made a list of foods discovered growing wild in the Americas and slowly domesticated, corn would not be on it. It wouldn't exist if it weren't for the natives of the Americas. Corn was essentially invented by humans, then cultivated and developed through the stages of its evolution as a crop and as a staple food. Most scholars believe the people of central Mexico developed what was then called maize at least 7,000 years ago, starting from a very different-looking wild grass called *teosinte*. The kernels were tiny and far apart, instead of pressed all together in the familiar neat rows. Over time, Indians throughout both South and North America came to depend on maize as one of their main nutritional sources, as evidenced by the foods of the pueblo cultures of the American Southwest. By about 1,000 years ago, cultivation of the crop had made it as far north as the eastern woodlands of New England. When Columbus introduced America to Europe and other Europeans came to settle it, corn was one of the first native foods they embraced for survival. While sweet potatoes, cranberry sauce and pumpkin pie were not part of the first Thanksgiving meal in 1621, corn surely would have been. The word "corn" can be traced to an Indo-European word that meant "small nugget," with variations evolving into the Germanic "korn" for any cereal grain and the Latin *granum* (grain), which also refers to any edible grass seed. When English and German settlers arrived in the New World, they referred to the crop as "corn," again meaning something generic. They distinguished it from other grains by calling it "Indian corn."

QUINOA FALAFEL

2 cans garbanzo beans, drained

1 small onion, roughly chopped

4 cloves garlic

2 teaspoons crushed red pepper

4 teaspoons ground cumin

2 teaspoons baking powder

4 tablespoons all-purpose flour

2 teaspoons salt

½ teaspoon black pepper

6 tablespoons chopped fresh parsley

¼ cup cooked quinoa

Corn oil for deep frying

QUINOA IS A SUPERFOOD OF THE AMERICAS. FALAFEL IS TRADITIONALLY MADE WITH ONLY GROUND CHICK PEAS, BUT WE REALLY LIKE WHAT HAPPENS WHEN YOU ADD THE QUINOA. WE COOK THE NUTTY-TASTING GRAIN AND KEEP IT WHOLE, BOTH FOR APPEARANCE AND TEXTURE. AS MORE AND MORE PEOPLE APPRECIATE, QUINOA IS A COMPLETE PROTEIN THAT'S EXTREMELY HIGH IN FIBER. THESE FRIED LATIN-MEDITERRANEAN FRITTERS ARE PERFECT POPPED BY THEMSELVES, OR AS SANDWICH ON A TORTILLA OR IN A PITA POCKET.

Combine all ingredients except the quinoa and oil in a food processor with a steel blade. Pulse until mixture is coarsely ground and transfer to a large mixing bowl. Fold in the cooked quinoa. Cover the bowl and refrigerate for about 2 hours. When ready to fry, form the mixture into pecan-sized balls and press out into a patty. Heat 4 inches of oil to 375° F in a deep fryer. Fry about 6 falafel at a time in the oil until golden brown, about 4 minutes. Drain on paper towels. Serve immediately. Makes 10-12 servings.

PEANUTS
Peanuts began life in the Americas, probably Brazil or Peru, and spread across the region as far north as Mexico. Still, when they arrived as food in North America, they (along with the pods known as okra that eventually lent their tribal name to gumbo) were among the few, much-treasured possessions of African slaves. Many in the New World, therefore, came to think of peanuts as imports from Africa. But at least as far back as 3,500 years ago, the indigenous peoples of South America made pottery shaped like peanuts and decorated their pots with peanut shapes. In a development similar to the ancient Egyptians in their pyramids, the Incas along the dry western coastline of their continent buried their dead with jars full of peanuts—nourishment for the long journey through the afterlife. The Spaniards encountered peanuts during their conquests and carried them back to Europe, from which they were spread by traders to Asia and especially to Africa. Over time, the peanut became known in African tribal religions as one of only a handful of plants to possess a soul. Once transported to the American South, slaves planted peanuts beginning in the late 1700s, calling them initially nguba (which inspired the slang word "goober") and eventually groundnuts, ground peas and finally peanuts. Peanuts attained a reputation as food for the poor until around 1900, growing steadily in popularity throughout the 20th century. As many know, African-American botanist George Washington Carver was their greatest champion.

ZUCCHINI-CASHEW MADELEINES

BOTH THE MAIN INGREDIENTS IN THIS DISH ARE NATIVE TO THE AMERICAS, SO IT FITS OUR FAMILY'S FOOD PHILOSOPHY PERFECTLY TO TRANSFORM A FRENCH CLASSIC BY USING THEM. YOU'LL RECOGNIZE THE CONCEPT OF THE MADELEINE HERE, BUT WE THINK THESE INGREDIENTS MAKE IT EVEN BETTER.

Preheat the oven to 350° F. In a large bowl, combine the sugar, eggs and vanilla. Stir in the zucchini, cashew pieces and melted butter. In a separate bowl, mix together the flour, baking soda, cinnamon and nutmeg. Stir these dry ingredients into the zucchini-cashew mixture along with the raisins. Coat a muffin-type pan with square shapes (like financiers) with cooking spray and divide the batter evenly, filling the spaces completely.

Bake until the bites are golden brown and the tops spring back when you press them down, 15-20 minutes. Test with a long toothpick or bamboo skewer, which will come out clean when bites are done. Set on a wire rack to cool for 5 minutes, then remove from the pan and let cool for another 20 minutes. Makes about 36.

1 ⅓ cup granulated sugar
2 eggs, lightly beaten
2 teaspoons vanilla extract
3 cups shredded zucchini
1 cup broken-up cashew pieces
¾ cup melted butter
3 cups all-purpose flour
2 teaspoons baking soda
2 teaspoon ground cinnamon
½ teaspoon ground nutmeg
1 cup California raisins

CASHEW

Known primarily as the wonderful kidney-shaped nut, the cashew is a native of Brazil. Its siblings in the family *Anacardium occidentale* include the mango, the pistachio and poison ivy. The tree, the fruit and the nut that hangs as a seed underneath might, in fact, have remained a Brazilian treasure forever, had it not been for some enterprising Portuguese sailors, who transported it from one of their colonies to another far away. Thus, cashews came to be associated not only with Brazil in South America but, beginning in the 16th century, with the state in India called Goa. To this day, as with many European food "immigrants" from the Americans, some people think of cashews as being from India. Unlike most fruits, whose seed is found at the center, cashew seeds hang from the bottom of cashew apples. The apples themselves are delicious but tend to be available only in the areas they are grown, as they start fermenting within 24 hours of being picked. They are, therefore, a local-only delicacy. They sometimes break out of the cycle a little by being preserved in jars and canned, or fermented (finished the work nature begins) as liqueurs. Meanwhile, cashew nuts get broken out of two hard shells and the caustic, black *cardol* in between that causes blistering of the skin, and shipped off to us.

STUFFED QUAIL TAQUITOS

8 quail breasts

¼ cup pineapple juice

1 tablespoon soy sauce

8 cremini mushrooms

3 tablespoons chimichurri
(see recipe p. 140)

½ shallot, minced

1 teaspoon corn oil

2 tablespoons seeded and
diced jalapeno

2 tablespoons diced red
bell pepper

2 tablespoons cotija cheese

1 tablespoon finely chopped basil

16 slices bacon

8 flour tortillas

Brown Butter Bearnaise
(see recipe p. 141)

GARNISH

Finely chopped romaine lettuce

Cotija cheese

Diced red bell pepper

Finely chopped basil

THIS FAVORITE CAME WITH THE OPENING OF THE FIRST AMERICAS, AND IT'S AN EXCELLENT NOD TO TEXAS. AT THE HEART OF IT ALL IS TRADITIONAL FRENCH BÉARNAISE, BUT IT SHOWS UP ON A TORTILLA TOPPED WITH BACON WRAPPED TEXAS QUAIL. BASIL AND TARRAGON BRING A HEADY HERBAL NOTE TO THE BASE OF BACON AND BEARNAISE.

Marinate the quail breasts 30 minutes in a bowl with the pineapple juice and soy. Remove the stem from each mushroom to create a cavity for stuffing, then brush the mushroom caps with chimichurri and grill briefly. Mince the mushroom stems and sauté with the shallot in the corn oil. Let cool, and make a duxelles by finely chopping mixture.

Preheat oven to 400° F. In a bowl, combine the cooled duxelle with the jalapeno, red bell pepper, cotija and basil and use to stuff each mushroom cap. Set 1 marinated quail breast on top of each mushroom and wrap each with 2 slices of bacon crossing each other. Set the quail packets seam-side down on a roasting pan and roast in oven for 18 minutes. Let cool enough to handle.

Meanwhile, spray the tortillas with cooking spray and cook lightly on one side in a pan or on a griddle, letting then turn golden and puffy. Slice each quail packet into 4-5 slices. Spread each tortilla with some Brown Butter Bearnaise and set the quail slices on top. Garnish with chopped romaine and the same flavors as the stuffing: cotija, red bell pepper and basil. Makes 8 taquitos.

CAVIAR TWINKIES

1 loaf brioche

½ stick unsalted butter

½ cup mascarpone cheese

2 ounces American paddlefish caviar

Fresh dill for garnish

I FIRST DID THIS HORS D'OEUVRE FOR MY DAD'S BIRTHDAY AT AMÉRICAS AND NOW IT HAS BECOME A MAINSTAY OF OUR CATERING MENUS. THE FIRST ENCOUNTERED A SAVORY VERSION SERVED ALONGSIDE A CAESAR SALAD, KIND OF LIKE A STUFFED CROUTON. IT DIDN'T TAKE MORE THAN THAT ONE ENCOUNTER TO INSPIRE A VARIATION AS A VEHICLE FOR AMERICAN PADDLEFISH CAVIAR. THE MASCARPONE FILLING NICELY BALANCES THE SALTINESS OF THE CAVIAR.

Slice the brioche into ½-inch slices and then cut each slice into 8 sticks. Melt the butter in a large saute pan and toast the brioche sticks in the butter until crispy and golden brown on all sides. Drain on paper towels and let cool enough to handle. Use a chopstick to hollow out a lengthwise hole inside the brioche sticks. Using a pastry bag, fill each hole with mascarpone. Spread a small amount of caviar on the end of each stick. Garnish with sprigs of fresh dill. Makes about 32.

SMOKED LAMB LOLLICHOPS

A PERUVIAN TRADITIONAL STREET FOOD CALLED *ANTICUCHO*—MADE WITH SKEWERS OF GRILLED BEEF HEART—TEMPTED US TO TRY USING SMALL, TENDER LAMB CHOPS INSTEAD. WE'VE FOUND THAT NOT ONLY IS THIS ONE OF OUR MOST POPULAR CREATIONS BUT THAT, BETWEEN THE VINEGAR-BASED MARINADE AND THE SMOKING, THE EFFECT IS REMINISCENT OF GOOD CAROLINA BARBECUE.

Prepare the Anticucho Marinade by whisking all ingredients together in a bowl. For the lollichops, with the racks still whole, cut off the fat cap and use a sharp knife to press all the meat downward toward the end, keeping it connecting. The result is a series of 8 bones connected by a panel of meat at one end. Season with salt and pepper, then brush with chimichurri. Smoke using a stovetop smoker and corn husks, exactly like the Corn-Smoked Crab Fingers (page 50).

Slice downward through the meat to separate individual chops. Coat with additional chimichurri and grill over high heat 4-5 minutes per side. About ¾ of the way through, brush the chops several types with the Anticucho Marinade, letting it cook on to form a red glaze. Let rest before serving. Makes 16 lollichops.

ANTICUCHO MARINADE

¼ cup panca pepper paste

½ cup unseasoned rice vinegar

2 tablespoons corn oil

½ teaspoon salt

½ teaspoon black pepper

½ teaspoon ground cumin

2 racks New Zealand lamb chops (16 chops)

Salt and pepper

½ cup chimichurri (see recipe p. 140)

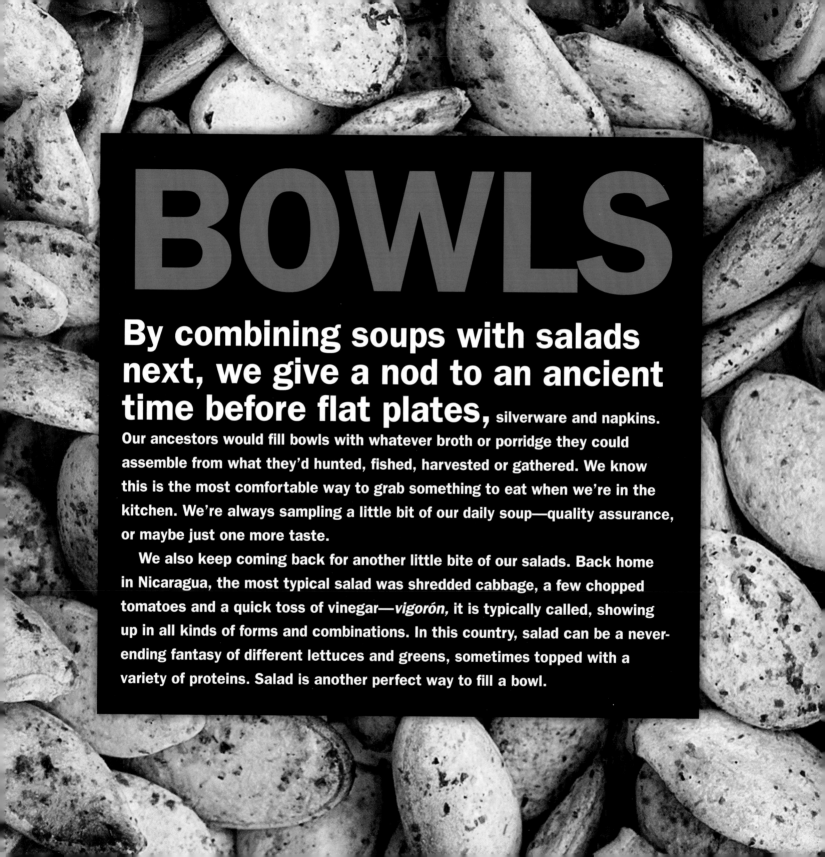

BOWLS

By combining soups with salads next, we give a nod to an ancient time before flat plates, silverware and napkins. Our ancestors would fill bowls with whatever broth or porridge they could assemble from what they'd hunted, fished, harvested or gathered. We know this is the most comfortable way to grab something to eat when we're in the kitchen. We're always sampling a little bit of our daily soup—quality assurance, or maybe just one more taste.

We also keep coming back for another little bite of our salads. Back home in Nicaragua, the most typical salad was shredded cabbage, a few chopped tomatoes and a quick toss of vinegar—*vigorón,* it is typically called, showing up in all kinds of forms and combinations. In this country, salad can be a never-ending fantasy of different lettuces and greens, sometimes topped with a variety of proteins. Salad is another perfect way to fill a bowl.

CAESAR SALAD

DRESSING

2 egg yolks

1 teaspoon Worcestershire sauce

¾ tablespoon lime juice

2-3 anchovy fillets

2-3 cloves garlic

1 teaspoons salt

1 tablespoon Dijon mustard

½ teaspoon white wine vinegar

½ cup grated Parmesan cheese

1 cup olive oil

Ciabatta bread, sliced or cut into cubes

1 tablespoon olive oil

Salt to taste

2 hearts of Romaine

¼ cup shredded Parmesan cheese

4 wedges lemon, grilled (optional)

CAESAR SALAD WAS CREATED BY AN ITALIAN RUNNING A RESTAURANT IN TIJUANA ACROSS THE BORDER FROM SAN DIEGO. THE AMERICAS HAVE ALWAYS BEEN HOME TO SUCH MIXING OF PEOPLES, CULTURES AND FOOD IDEAS. WE LIKE OUR CAESAR DRESSING A LITTLE THICKER THAN SOME VERSIONS, SINCE WE ENJOY THIS SALAD TOSSED THE WAY CAESAR CARDINI DID IT AND ALSO WITH THE DRESSING AS A DIJON-ANCHOVY-GARLIC DIP FOR THE ROMAINE LEAVES.

Prepare the Caesar dressing by combining all the ingredients except the oil in a food processor. Mix well for 2 minutes, then slowly add oil while processing until emulsified. Prepare the ciabatta croutons by heating olive oil in a pan and toasting until golden brown on the outside, warm but still soft on the inside. Remove from pan and lightly season with salt.

For traditional presentation, chop the Romaine hearts, toss with the dressing and Parmesan, and serve with croutons. Or, for a more interesting visual impact, peel the individual leaves from the Romaine hearts, brush each leaf with the dressing, then reassemble to look like the original heart. Serve with croutons on the side and a sprinkling of Parmesan cheese. Serves 4.

BUTTERNUT SQUASH

There is evidence that some sort of gourds were cultivated and probably eaten, farther back than the ancient Egyptians—who built pyramids as tombs, rather than as ceremonial places the way the Aztecs and Maya of the Americas did. In fact, some gourds were found buried alongside the masters of those tombs, reflecting their great value. Botanically named *Curcurbita moschata*, the family includes butternut squash, with buttery orange flesh and sweet taste, as well as pumpkin and zucchini. Native Americans, especially in Guatemala and Mexico, once believed squash was so nutritious that, like the Egyptians, they buried it along with the dead to provide them nourishment on their final journey. Despite the wonderful flavors we get from the butternut variety today, especially when it's roasted, squash was originally grown for the seeds. They were planted near homes because the proximity was thought to increase fertility. Later versions of the plant produced fruit that had a thicker skin, fewer seeds and less waste. The vegetable was not introduced to Europe before the Columbus era and was not commonly consumed until the 19th century.

ROMAINE AND GOAT CHEESE SPEARS WITH CANDIED PECANS

CANDIED PECANS

4 cups crushed pecan

1 cup powdered sugar

1 ½ teaspoon ground red pepper

1 teaspoon salt

½ gallon corn oil for frying

RASPBERRY DILL VINAIGRETTE

½ cup diced onion

½ cup malt vinegar

¼ cup karo syrup

¾ raspberry purée

1 tablespoon raspberry liqueur such as Chambord

1 ½ tablespoon sesame oil

1 teaspoon salt

12 leaves baby romaine

4 tablespoons crumbled goat cheese

1 teaspoon chopped dill

THIS SALAD IS A BIT UNIQUE, ESPECIALLY SINCE IT'S MEANT TO BE FOLDED AND EATEN WITH YOUR HANDS. THE DISTINCT, MILDLY SOUR TASTE OF THE GOAT CHEESE IS PERFECTLY BALANCED BY THE SWEETNESS OF THE RASPBERRY DRESSING. THE CANDIED PECANS PROVIDE A TOUCH OF TEXAS AND A WELCOME SWEET-HOT CRUNCH.

First, candy the pecans. Bring ½ gallon of water to a boil and blanch the nuts briefly, then drain through a fine sieve until cool and dry. In a large mixing bowl, combine the powdered sugar, red pepper and salt. Pour the pecans into this mixture and turn with your hands until thoroutghly coated. Heat the oil in a large pan to 350º F. Fry pecans in the oil for 1 minute, being careful not to let them burn. Spread them on a baking sheet to cool. You will have leftover pecans.

Prepare the dressing by combining the diced onion in the vinegar and letting it sit for at least an hour. In a food processor, purée the onion and vinegar until smooth, then pour in the syrup, purée and liqueur. When the mixture is smooth and the speed is on high, slowly pour in the sesame oil to make the dressing emulsify. Season with salt. Makes about 2 cups.

Build the salad like a series of tacos, spreading each romaine leaf with some dressing then topping that with grumbled goat cheese followed by candied pecans. Sprinkle with chopped dill. Serves 4.

CAPRICHOSA

CAPRICHOSA IS SPANISH FOR CAPRICIOUS OR FICKLE OR INCONSTANT, WE LIKE THAT EVERY BITE OF THIS SALAD IS DIFFERENT, DEPENDING ON HOW YOU ASSEMBLE EACH BITE OF AVOCADO, TOMATO, MOZZARELLA AND CRAB ON THIS TARE ON A CAPRESE.

In a mixing bowl, combine the crabmeat with the Jalapeno Remoulade, basil and tarragon, folding gently to moisten without breaking up the crab. Season with salt and pepper. On a plate, form a version on a traditional Insalata Caprese by alternating 3 slices of tomato with 2 slices of jalapeno, leaning like dominos. Divide crab salad equally over each of the 4 toasted croissants, set beside the Caprese and decorate with a sliced avocado half. Garnish with additional chopped basil and drizzle with olive oil. Serves 4.

½ pound jumbo jump crabmeat

2 ½ tablespoons Jalapeno Remoulade (see recipe p. 90)

2 ¼ tablespoons finely chopped basil

¾ teaspoon finely chopped tarragon

Salt and pepper

4 Roma tomatoes, peeled and seeded, each sliced into 3 pieces

8 slices fresh mozzarella

4 pressed and toasted croissants

2 avocados, halved and sliced

Additional chopped basil

Olive oil

AVOCADO

The avocado *(Persea gratissima)* gets its name from the Nahuatl word ahuacatl meaning "testicle," a reference to its shape. The oldest evidence of avocado use was found in a cave located in Coxcatlán, Puebla, Mexico, dating from around 10,000 BC. A water jar shaped like an avocado, dating back to 900 A.D., was discovered in the pre-Incan city of Chan Chan. Spanish explorers discovered the Aztecs enjoying avocados but were hardly impressed by their mild flavor. The Aztecs used them primarily as a sexual stimulant, following the ancient wisdom that anything that looked sexual was likely to improve sex. It was the Spanish who brought the avocado to the English, who no doubt preferred not to think about its original application. Avocado took on its more pronounceable name thanks to England's Sir Henry Sloane in 1669, and appeared in print in America less than three decades later. The first Florida crops were credited to horticulturist Henry Perrine, who planted groves in 1833. However, avocados did not become a commercial crop in the United States until the early 20th century, with a major assist from growers in California.

CHINITA CHICKEN SALAD

Corn oil for deep frying

1 pound ground chicken breast

1 ½ tablespoons cornstarch

1 egg white, lightly beaten

1 ½ tablespoons corn oil

1 ½ tablespoons fresh minced garlic

⅓ pound jicama, diced

Fried rice noodles

CHINITA SAUCE

¼ cup minced garlic

¼ cup minced fresh ginger

1 ½ cup soy sauce

⅓ cup thick soy sauce

1 ¼ cup white vinegar

2 tablespoons rice vinegar

1 ½ cup sugar

1 ⅓ cup chicken stock

THIS COOLING DISH DELIVERS GREAT TEXTURES FROM THE CRISPY RICE NOODLES AND DICED JICAMA AND ADDS A KICK OF SWEET HEAT WITH THE CHILI SAUCE.

Heat the oil in a deep pan 350° F. In a bowl, combine the chicken with the cornstarch, egg white and 1 ½ tablespoons corn oil. Mix well by hand until chicken is evenly coated, then transfer to the hot oil. Stir with a slotted spoon to break up clumps. Drain the chicken through a sieve.

Place the Chinita Sauce (see recipe below) in a large sauté pan, along with the minced garlic, jicama and drained chicken. Stirfry until sauce is reduced and thickened. Remove from heat and serve topped with crispy rice noodles. Serves 4.

CHINITA SAUCE

Make the Chinita Sauce by combining all ingredients in a large stainless-steel mixing bowl, whisking until smooth.

SWEET PEPPERS

The phrase "It all started with Columbus" can certainly be applied to the not-hot peppers sometimes referred to as "bell." And in this instance, it wouldn't apply at all to their cultivation but to their misleading name. Peppers are native to Mexico, Central America and northern South America. The seeds were later carried to Spain in 1493 and from there spread to other European, African and Asian countries. Columbus himself called the fruits "peppers" when he brought them back to Europe, perhaps hoping to associate them with peppercorns, the fruit of Piper nigrum, an unrelated plant originating from India and then a highly prized condiment. At that time, the name "pepper" was applied in Europe to all known spices with a hot and pungent taste and naturally extended to the newly discovered Capsicum. The alternative word chile has origins in Mexico, from the Nahuatl term *chilli* or *xilli*. The bell pepper is a member of the *Capsicum* genus, but it is the only *Capsicum* that does not produce capcaicin, a chemical that can cause a strong burning sensation when it comes in contact with the mucous membranes in the mouth. In simple terms, then, sweet peppers are not hot. The shape-reference "bell pepper" is often used, though the whole Columbus confusion comes back for seconds in Australia and New Zealand, where the inoffensive fruit is called "capsicum." Today, with their tangy taste, crunchy texture and vivid colors ranging from green, red, yellow, orange, purple, brown to black, sweet peppers are sometimes called "the Christmas ornaments of the vegetable world."

CORN POBLANO SOUP

1 cup chopped poblano peppers

2 tablespoons corn oil

5 cups whole kernel corn

½ cup diced onion

1 teaspoon minced garlic

½ teaspoon crushed red pepper

1 quart whole milk

2 cups heavy cream

2 tablespoons chicken stock, concentrated

2 ½ tablespoons cornstarch

2 ½ tablespoons water

WHEN THIS SOUP IS ON, IT'S A GOOD DAY FOR GUESTS AND STAFF ALIKE. CORN IS ONE OF THE MOST PROFOUNDLY AMERICAN OF ALL INGREDIENTS. HERE WE GIVE IT A TOASTED-NUTTY FLAVOR ON TOP OF ITS NATURAL SWEETNESS BY CHARRING AND PEELING. POBLANO PEPPERS AND THE GARNISH OF PUMPKIN SEEDS LEAVE NO DOUBT OF ITS HERITAGE.

Char poblano peppers over a stone burner; shock in a bowl of water and ice. Peel off skins and remove seeds. Heat corn oil over high heat in a large soup pot, then sauté corn, peppers, onion and garlic until lightly caramelized. Add the milk, heavy cream and concentrated chicken stock. Cook over medium heat for 10 minutes.

Remove soup from the heat and blend until smooth in a blender or food processor. Return to low heat and simmer for 10 minutes. Bring just to a low boil. Dissolve the cornstarch in the water to form a slurry; stir into the soup. Once the soup starts to thicken, reduce heat and simmer 10-15 minutes. Add salt to taste. Strain through a fine sieve. Serves 4-6.

CHILE PEPPERS

In the history of Latin cooking, especially as understood and enjoyed in the United States, few foods of the Americas have been as extravagantly praised or as extravagantly damned as the chile pepper. The debate seems to be eternal, about whether this or that dish "has flavor" or is "just hot." Without a doubt, however, chile peppers of varying degrees of heat came to be popular because they delivered a flavor lots of people liked. Members of the *capsicum* family have been a part of the human diet in the Americas since at least 7,500 BC. There is archaeological evidence in southwestern Ecuador that peppers were domesticated more than 6,000 years ago. Columbus was one of the first Europeans to encounter them, during his 1493 return voyage to the Caribbean. He called them "peppers" because they, like peppercorns on the *Piper* family, have a spicy taste. Chiles quickly became botanical curiosities in Spanish and Portuguese monasteries in Europe. The prominence of chile peppers in most Asian cuisine is probably a legacy of the Portuguese, who encountered them in Lisbon and promoted them along the spice routes they dominated with Arab traders. Chiles traveled from Portuguese Goa in India (where they figured in *vindaloo*, a fiery local spin on a Portuguese dish) all the way through Central Asia and Turkey to Hungary, where they gave birth to the Hungarian national spice paprika.

BLACK BEAN GUMBO

HOUSTON IS VERY CLOSE TO LOUISIANA, AND WITH HURRICANES, THE OIL & GAS INDUSTRY, FAMILY AND FUN, THE TWO PLACES HAVE A REGULAR AND PROFOUND POPULATION EXCHANGE. OVER THE YEARS, OUR FAMILY HAS ENJOYED THE LOYALTY OF MANY GUESTS WHO CALL THAT INTRIGUING LAND ON THE FAR SIDE OF THE SABINE RIVER HOME. THEY BEGGED US TO MAKE GUMBO. IT REFLECTS OUR LATIN POINT-OF-VIEW WITH THE EARTHY ADDITION OF BLACK BEAN.

Make a roux by combining the flour and butter in a large pot over medium-high heat and stirring until the mixture is a toasted tan color. In another large pot or Dutch oven, sauté the onion, celery, bell pepper and garlic in the oil until transparent. Add the black pepper, crushed red peppers, thyme and oregano, stirring to continue cooking. Add this mixture to the roux.

Add water, shrimp stock, fish granules and Kitchen Bouquet to the black bean sauce. Bring to a boil, reduce heat and simmer 15 minutes. Add black bean sauce and file powder to the gumbo and bring to a boil. Once gumbo lightly coats the back of a spoon, remove from heat and let cool enough to purée in a blender until smooth. Return to heat. Coat the fish in a marinade of the egg white, cornstarch, sherry and soy, then fry in a little oil. Break into pieces with a fork and add to the gumbo, along with the shrimp and crabmeat. Heat through. Serve in bowls over white rice. Serves 10-12.

½ cup all-purpose flour
⅓ cup unsalted butter
1 cup diced onion
1 cup diced celery
1 cup diced green bell pepper
2 teaspoons minced garlic
3 tablespoons corn oil
1 teaspoon black pepper
1 teaspoon crushed red pepper
1 teaspoon thyme
1 teaspoon oregano
2 cups water
4 cups shrimp stock
1 teaspoon hon dashi fish stock granules
1 tablespoon Kitchen Bouquet
1 cup spicy black bean sauce (see recipe on p. 122)
¼ teaspoon filé powder
Salt to taste
½ pound snapper
1 egg white
1 tablespoon cornstarch
1 tablespoon sherry
1 tablespoon soy sauce
½ pound peeled and deveined shrimp, poached or boiled
½ pound jumbo lump crabmeat
Cooked white rice

IDIAZABAL CHEESE SOUP

2 ½ cups smoked and grated idiazabal cheese

2 cups chicken stock

1 cup beef stock

½ cup heavy cream

2 tablespoons cornstarch

2 tablespoons water

4 poached eggs

IF THE WORD "IDIAZABAL" STRIKES YOU AS HARD TO SAY, THAT'S PROBABLY BECAUSE THIS DELICIOUS NUTTY SMOKY SHEEP'S MILK CHEESE COMES FROM THE BASQUE REGION OF SPAIN. HOWEVER DIFFICULT THE PRONUNCIATION IS, THE END RESULT WILL PLEASE THE MANY FANS OF *HUEVOS RANCHEROS,* AS THE POACHED EGG PROVIDES A SWIRL OF LIQUID YOLK THAT TIES ALL THE FLAVORS TOGETHER.

Combine all ingredients in a pot over medium high heat, whisking briskly to melt the cheese. Raise the heat and bubble for 3-4 minutes. Dissolve the cornstarch in the water and add, stirring to thicken. Top each bowl with a poached egg. Serves 4.

IN TRIBUTE
Gumaro Lopez

Gumaro was our first hire at the original Churrascos, and to this day he remains one of our most important. Of course he's a hard worker, as the people who stay with our company always are. And of course he has talents in the kitchen, for we would accept nothing less. But as the first person we brought on, when he knew so much and we knew so little, he became my teacher in a way I'll never forget. Though he came to Houston from northern Mexico, he had also spent seven years working with a classically trained French chef at a place called La Tour d'Argent—and he had learned his lessons well. Before long, I knew all the most important French techniques and started incorporating them into my thinking about Latin food. Even better, Gumaro and I became a team. I didn't have to apply French technique. I could simply think of some Latin taste, some Latin ingredient, some Latin dish I loved, and he could take it from there. Part of the fun was that he was learning from me too, since virtually none of these Latin flavors existed in the desert where he grew up. There were several older chefs in that first Churrascos kitchen, and some of them were upset when I named Gumaro our head chef. It's a decision I've never regretted.

SOPA CUBANA

2 pounds dry black beans

1 ½ gallon water

1 bay leaf

½ cup whole garlic cloves

2 cups chopped onion

¼ cup chopped green pepper

2 tablespoons salt

1 ½ tablespoons ground cumin

1 ½ tablespoons black pepper

1 tablespoon crushed red pepper

⅔ cup tomato paste

⅓ cup red wine

½ pound smoked ham, cubed

½ pound unsalted butter

12 bread bowls

MANY BEAN DISHES FROM LATIN AMERICA HAVE FOUND A MUCH WIDER AUDIENCE. IN THE PAST COUPLE OF DECADES, THE BLACK BEAN SOUP ENJOYED IN CUBA HAS BECOME A STAPLE FAR BEYOND THE CARIBBEAN. WE LIKE TO SERVE THE SOUP IN A HOLLOWED-OUT LOAF OF ROUND, CRUSTY BREAD, A TREATMENT USUALLY RESERVED FOR CLAM CHOWDER AND OTHER SUBSTANTIAL NEW ENGLAND SOUPS THAT INVITE THE GUEST TO EAT IT BOWL AND ALL.

Combine the beans, water, bay leaf and garlic cloves in a large soup pot and bring to a boil, then reduce heat and cook until beans are tender, about 1 ½ hours. Stir in the onion and bell pepper along with all the seasonings. Add the tomato paste and red wine, stirring to fully incorporate. Cook for 30 minutes, then stir in the cubed ham and the butter. Remove the bay leaf and crush the garlic cloves with a spoon. Serve hot into bowls created by hollowing out round loaves of bread. Serves 12.

CHUPE DE LANGOSTA

IN PERU, *CHUPE* MAY SOUND LIKE THE ENGLISH WORD "SOUP," BUT IT'S ACTUALLY MORE LIKE A THICK, NOURISHING BISQUE. IT'S TRADITIONALLY MADE WITH ALL KINDS OF SHELLFISH—WHATEVER IS AVAILABLE FRESH—BUT NO FINFISH. HIGHLIGHTS OF THIS VERSION INCLUDE THE GRILLED CORN AND THE SMOKED PANELA CHEESE, BOTH OF WHICH ADD AN INTENSE, OUTDOOR-CHAR FLAVOR.

Combine the rinsed lobster shells with the oil in a very large pan and sauté over medium-high heat until a dark brown crust forms on the bottom, about 15 minutes. Add the vegetables, garlic, seasonings and rice, cooking for 15 minutes and stirring occasionally. Add tomato paste and stir for 10 minutes. Pour in sherry and water to deglaze, scraping up browned bits from bottom of the pan. Add water to cover shells, if necessary.

Simmer until liquid is reduced by ½, 40-50 minutes. Strain out the shells and vegetables, then strain through a fine sieve into a saucepot. Add the cornstarch slurry and bring to a boil to thicken. Add cream and cook briefly. Pour chupe into bowls over cooked seafood, grilled corn kernels and cubes of smoked panela. Serves 8-10.

5 pounds lobster shells, rinsed
¼ cup corn oil
1 ½ cup chopped onion
1 cup chopped carrot
1 cup chopped celery
⅓ cup chopped garlic
1 ½ teaspoon dried oregano
1 ½ teaspoon black pepper
1 bay leaf
½ cup uncooked jasmine rice
1 cup tomato paste
2 cups dry sherry
2 gallons water
½ cup cornstarch dissolved in ½ cup water
1 cup heavy cream
Cooked seafood, including chunks of lobster from shells
Grilled corn kernels
Cubes of smoked panela cheese

PUMPKIN
The pumpkin has found its way into the heart of American tradition. Though its name is Greek (*pepōn,* for large melon), both it and its uses are native to the tribes that lived primarily in the American Northeast before the arrival of the Pilgrims. Dating back to a first mention in 1547, the English term pumpion or pompion was quickly applied. It was one of the many foods used by natives in this part of the New World. As a staple food, pumpkins helped the Native Americans make it through long, cold winters. They used the sweet flesh in numerous ways: roasted, baked, parched, boiled and dried. They ate pumpkin seeds and also used them as a medicine. The blossoms were added to stews. Dried pumpkin could be stored and ground into flour. It's worth remembering that these early pumpkins were not the traditional round orange upright fruit we think of today. They were a crooked neck variety. Archeologists have determined that variations of squash and pumpkins were cultivated along river and creek banks with sunflowers and beans long before the emergence of maize (corn). After that, ancient farmers learned to grow squash with maize and beans using the "Three Sisters" tradition, one of history's earliest attempts at sustainable agriculture. Corn served as the natural trellis for the beans, and the beans roots set nitrogen in the soil to nourish the corn. The bean vines helped stabilize the corn stalks, and the pumpkin plants sheltered the shallow roots of the corn. The Pilgrims embraced the sweet, multi-purpose fruit, which of course became a traditional Thanksgiving food.

CHICKEN AND YUCA DUMPLING SOUP

ALBONDIGAS

2 ¼ pounds ground chicken

⅔ cup chopped onion

½ cup chopped green pepper

1 teaspoon chopped garlic

½ cup chopped cilantro

1 egg

1 ½ teaspoon salt

1 ½ teaspoon Creole seasoning

1 pound boiled yuca

SOUP

¼ cup corn oil

2 ½ cup chopped onion

1 ½ teaspoon minced garlic

2 ½ cup diced tomatoes

2 canned chipotle peppers
in adobo, minced

½ cup white wine

1 gallon chicken stock

2 tablespoons lime juice

1 tablespoon salt

1 tablespoon black pepper

GARNISH

4 avocados, diced

Fried tortilla strips

Chopped cilantro

Cotija cheese

THIS IS THE CLOSEST THING WE DO IN OUR RESTAURANTS TO CHICKEN TORTILLA SOUP, WHICH SO MANY DINERS HAVE GROWN TO LOVE. WHEN WE CONTEMPLATED OUR OWN VERSION, WHAT WE THOUGHT OF WAS NOT CHUNKS OR SLIVERS OF CHICKEN BUT MEATBALLS. MORE LIKE DUMPLINGS, THEY'RE A PERFECT BALANCE OF GROUND CHICKEN AND YUCA. WE LOVE THE WAY THE YUCA MAKES THEM PUFF AS THEY COOK.

Preheat oven to 350° F. In a food processor, combine the chicken with the vegetables, egg and seasoning, processing until a thick, smooth dough develops. Add the yuca a little at a time, processing to thoroughly incorporate. Use a scoop that produces small meatballs about 1 rounded teaspoon. Bake in the oven for 12 minutes.

Heat the oil in a large pot and sauté the onion until starting to caramelize, then add the garlic and stir briefly. Add the tomatoes and chipotles, stirring for 1-2 minutes before adding the wine, stock, lime juice, salt and pepper. Cook for 20 minutes, then add the cooked meatballs. Serve in bowls. Top with diced avocado and garnish as desired with tortilla strips, cilantro and cotija. Serves 8-10.

FOIE GRAS AND MOREL SOUP

2 cups port wine

2 cups chicken stock

4 cups dried morel mushrooms

8 ounces duck foie gras,
cut in ½ inch cubes

4 cups heavy cream

3 tablespoons cornstarch

3 tablespoons water

1 teaspoon salt

IF THERE'S ANY DISH IN OUR RESTAURANTS THAT SCREAMS OVER-THE-TOP DECA-DENCE, THIS IS IT. THE RECIPE BEGAN AS A SAUCE AT ARTISTA, BUT EVOLVED FROM THERE. SURPRISINGLY, FOR ALL ITS RICH COMPONENTS, THIS SOUP IS STILL LIGHT ENOUGH THAT YOU'LL KEEP GOING BACK FOR ANOTHER SPOONFUL. AND IT STILL WORKS GREAT AS A SAUCE. WE LOVE IT ON CHICKEN, QUAIL OR DUCK.

In a pot, bring the port and the water to a boil, then pour over the dried mushrooms in a large bowl. Let them steep for 5 minutes to rehydrate. Strain the mushrooms, reserving them and the liquid separately. In a large saucepan, stir the cubes of foie gras until they start to brown and plenty of their fat is rendered. Add the port-water mixture, followed by the cream. Dissolve the cornstarch in the water and add to the pot, stirring until the soup thickens. Add the morels and heat through. Season with salt. Serves 4-6.

IN TRIBUTE
Luisino Sanchez

The chef we know as "Chele"—nobody around here calls him Luisino—came to Churrascos early on from working with Mark Cox (later of his own Mark's American Cuisine in Houston) when he was still with Tony Vallone. Tony's standards of cuisine are very high, with a solid foundation in French and an incredible specialization in the regional foods of Italy. Thus, we had two Mexican chefs: Gumaro an expert on French cooking and Chele an expert on Italian. Chefs always understand the importance of foundations, and both of these men brought solid foundations to their new adventure with me, as we explored a vast and diverse Latin America neither of them knew much about. Chele has a terrific work ethic and tre-mendous loyalty to our family and to any restaurant we create. Plus, he's not one of those tyrant-diva chefs that so many talented people become these days. He puts out awesome food at great volume, and he does it in a collegial, fun way, which makes him perfect for a Cordúa kitchen.

SMALL
Plates

With our Spanish ancestry, we were intrigued by the fact that today's all-American appetizers have much in common with the tapas so beloved in Spain. The tradition began as a sensible one: whenever someone ordered a glass of wine or spirits in a bar, the bartender also served a bite to eat. The little dishes the tapas came on were counted to determine how many drinks to put on the customer's bill. The food, of course, was free. In our kitchens, small plates provide us with the same sense of excitement and challenge that our perfect bites do: the necessity of saying a lot of wonderful things with food, fast. Our customers have started to realize this truth, becoming quite adventurous ordering appetizers. And we love it when they fill their table with lots of small plates. We believe food is always about sharing.

LOBSTER CAMPECHANA

SAUCE

¼ cup chopped green olives

⅓ cup extra-virgin olive oil

½ cup ketchup

¼ cup sriracha chile-garlic sauce

⅓ cup shrimp broth

⅓ cup jalapeno brine

¾ cup lime juice

1 ¼ cups lobster meat, torn into chunks

2 avocados, meat scooped and cut into chunks

1 ½ cups chopped cilantro

½ cup minced yellow onion

½ cup chopped Roma tomato

1 ½ teaspoons chopped jalapeno

1 ½ tablespoons lime juice

1 teaspoon salt

¼ cup pork chicharrones

THIS SEAFOOD FIREWORKS DISPLAY IS NAMED AFTER THE SHRIMP-RICH BAY OF CAMPECHE JUST OFF THE GULF BY TAMPICO, MEXICO. TEXANS GRABBED HOLD OF *CAMPECHANA* MADE WITH SHRIMP YEARS AGO, NOT LEAST BECAUSE IT SEEMED TO HELP WITH HANGOVERS. WHEN WE WENT LOOKING FOR OUR CAMPECHANA, HOWEVER, WE KNEW IT HAD TO BE MADE WITH SWEET LOBSTER MEAT INSTEAD OF SHRIMP. AND IT ENDED UP INCORPORATING MORE COMPLEXITY—FROM A BUILT-IN VERSION OF PERUVIAN *LECHE DE TIGRE* FOR CITRUSY SNAP TO VIETNAMESE *SRIRACHA* FOR A PUNCH OF SWEET-GARLICKY HEAT AND CHICHARRONES FOR CRUNCH. IF YOU EVER THOUGHT *CAMPECHANA* WAS JUST A SHRIMP COCKTAIL IN A SOMBRERO, THIS VERSION WILL CHANGE YOUR MIND.

In a blender or food processor, combine all the sauce ingredients until smooth. Pour the sauce into a bowl and combine with the lobster and avocado. Stir in the cilantro, onion, tomato, jalapeno, lime juice and salt. Let sit for about 10 minutes to let flavors meld. Serves with tortilla chips. Serves 8-10.

TOMATO

To hear some proud Virginians tell the tale, Thomas Jefferson single-handedly developed the tomato in his gardens at Monticello and then was generous enough to share it with the waiting world. To hear some proud Italians tell it, the tomato hailed from the place most associated with its cookery—the Italy of pizza, spaghetti, *insalata Caprese* and a thousand other great tomato recipes. The fact is, within the tangled web of the Age of Conquest, the tomato is an all-American fruit (not a vegetable, though it came to be used and thought of that way). And the hardest part of its journey was not making it all the way from the Aztecs of Mexico to Italy and finally back again; the hardest part was convincing most people it wasn't going to kill them. The very name tells us much about the fruit's ancient origins. *Tomatl* comes from Nahuatl, the language of the Aztecs, getting translated into the Latin-based languages of Europe as some version of *tomate* by the 17th century. Still, at the same time Europeans were falling for the beauty of both fruit and plant, they were associating it with members of the *Solancaea* family like henbane, mandrake and deadly nightshade—each as poisonous as it sounds. With their roots in England and Europe, most early Americans grew up believing the same thing. It was Jefferson who encountered the fruit during an agricultural foray into Italy and decided, based on its still-limited consumption there, it was good to eat. Jefferson's campaign enjoyed only limited success. It would take another century and a flourish of Italian immigrants now well-versed in tomato cookery to drive the New World wild for a fruit first enjoyed there.

TIRITAS

3 frozen calamari fillets, almost thawed

1 cup all-purpose flour

1 egg

1 cup milk

4 cups crushed potato chips

JALAPENO REMOULADE

3 cups mayonnaise

⅔ cup diced red bell pepper

⅔ cup diced onion

¼ cup diced green onion

1 tablespoon crushed red pepper

1 ½ tablespoons lime juice

1 ½ teaspoons salt

THE POTATO WAS BORN IN PERU, SO IN A SENSE THIS DISH WAS TOO—BUT IT'S BECOME EXTREMELY POPULAR HERE IN TEXAS. INSTEAD OF FAMILIAR CALAMARI RINGS OR TENTACLES, WE LIKE TO SLICE FINGER-FRIENDLY STRIPS OF PLEASANTLY CHEWY MEAT. WE USE POTATO CHIPS TO CONTRIBUTE A SNACK-CRACKY DELICIOUSNESS.

Preheat oil in a deep fryer to 350° F. Before the calamari are thawed completely, it will be easier to slice them into thin strips. Make an assembly line with bowls of flour, the egg beaten with the milk, and the crushed potato chips. Dredge the calamari strips in the flour and shake off excess, then dip them into the egg wash and finally into the potato chips. Cover them completely, pressing lightly to help the chips adhere. Deep fry the strips in batches until golden brown, only 1-2 minutes per batch. Drain on paper towels. Serve with Jalapeno Remoulade (see below).

JALAPENO REMOULADE

Combine all ingredients in a mixing bowl, whisking until smooth. Makes about 4 cups.

IN TRIBUTE
Frederico Espinoza

Now our company's director of operations, Fred started working for us because of unrest in his native Peru. He was studying to be an engineer in Lima when a bomb went off nearby, convincing him it might be a good idea to continue his studies in the States. While here in Houston at the University of St. Thomas, he came to work as a busboy at Churrascos. Odd as this may sound, at one point we held elections among the staff for manager positions. Instead of a bulldog from the owner watching over them, what I wanted was more a union leader who would express their concerns. Fred was one of those chosen by his peers. Later, we sponsored Fred when he went to earn his MBA from Rice University. To this day, I hold him up as an example of what good work can get you. It's an amazing story.

PALMITO CRAB CAKES

CRABCAKES HAVE BECOME OMNIPRESENT ON CONTEMPORARY MENUS. WITH THE CRUNCH SUPPLIED BY HEARTS OF PALM AND THE SMOOTH SWEETNESS OF THE AVOCADO MOUSSE, WE TAKE OUR CRAB CAKES IN A DIFFERENT DIRECTION WITH THE ADDITION OF HEART OF PALM AND PLANTAIN.

In a mixing bowl, combine the crabmeat and palmito with the bell pepper, green onion and Jalapeno Remoulade. Form into 3-inch patties about ½ inch high. Set in the refrigerator for 30 minutes. Meanwhile, set up an assembly line of bowls, one holding the flour, one the egg beaten into the milk and the last, the potato flakes.

Working smoothly, dredge the crab cakes in the flour and shake off excess, then into the egg wash and then into the potato flakes. Partially repeat by dipping in the egg wash again and back into the potato flakes, pressing lightly to help them adhere. (If you like, you can do up to this point an hour or two in advance and keep the crab cakes in the refrigerator.) Heat the oil in a deep fryer to 350° F. Fry the crab cakes till golden brown, 3-4 minutes. They can also be made half-size for use as an hors d'oeuvre. Serve with Avocado Mousse. Makes 4 cakes.

Note: The goal of shredding hearts of palm, known as palmitos in the Latin world, is to make them resemble flakes of crabmeat while retaining their pleasantly crunchy texture. To that end, be sure to choose of tender hearts of palm; those that seem dry and woody should be discarded. Shred them lengthways using a fork. At that point, it's easy to slice them sideways into short lengths.

AVOCADO MOUSSE

Combine all ingredients in a blender and purée until smooth. Makes about 1 pint.

¼ pound lump crabmeat

¼ cup shredded heart of palm

2 tablespoons diced red bell pepper

2 tablespoons diced green onion

¼ cup Jalapeno Remoulade (see recipe p. 90)

¼ cup all-purpose flour

1 egg

1 cup milk

½ cup instant potato flakes

Avocado Mousse (see below)

AVOCADO MOUSSE

3 avocados, peeled

1 teaspoon minced garlic

½ cup water

½ tablespoon kosher salt

2 tablespoons chopped red onion

2 tablespoon chopped cilantro

1 teaspoon chopped jalapeno

1 tablespoon fresh lime juice

SOFTSHELL CRAWFISH TAQUITOS

TEMPURA BATTER

1 cup all-purpose flour
½ cup cornstarch
2 teaspoons kosher salt
1 teaspoons baking powder
1 cup water
½ cup ice

2 tablespoons minced onion
1 tablespoons malt vinegar
12 softshell crawfish
12 4-inch flour tortillas
Melted butter or cooking spray
¼ cup hoisin sauce
2 tablespoons Jalapeno Remoulade (see recipe p. 90)
1 ½ cup shredded cabbage
1 ½ avocados, each cut into 8 slices
2 teaspoons sesame oil
2 tablespoons toasted sesame seeds
12 sprigs cilantro

ONE OF OUR FAMILY'S FAVORITE SUSHI PLACES IN HOUSTON, KOBE, STARTED DOING TEMPURA-FRIED SOFTSHELL CRAWFISH *NGIRI* A FEW YEARS AGO, AND WE WERE ENCHANTED. WE STILL ORDER IT THERE. WHEN WE OPENED ARTISTA AT THE HOBBY CENTER, WE KNEW WE HAD TO CREATE OUR OWN VERSION. SERVED ON A TAQUITO WITH AVOCADO, PICKLED CABBAGE AND ONION, TOASTED SESAME SEEDS AND *HOISIN* SAUCE, IT HAS BECOME A PRE-THEATER FAVORITE.

Prepare the tempura batter by combining the dry ingredients in a mixing bowl, then stirring in the water and the ice. Keep ice-cold. Mix the diced onion with the malt vinegar in a bowl. Coat the crawfish in the batter and fry until golden brown in 350° F corn oil. Keep warm in the oven. Coat the tortillas with butter or cooking spray, then heat them in a cast-iron skillet or nonstick pan.

In a clean open space, layout the warm tortillas. Squirt each tortilla with hoisin sauce followed by the Japaleno Remoulade, forming a crossways pattern. Toss the cabbage with the onion and malt vinegar and divide over the tortillas. Add 1 slice of avocado to each and top with the fried softshell crawfish. Drizzle with sesame oil and sprinkle with sesame seeds. Garnish each taquito with a sprig of cilantro. Makes 12.

JERUSALEM ARTICHOKE

In 2002, in the town of Nice on the French Riviera, the Festival for the Heritage of the French Cuisine voted the Jerusalem artichoke the "best soup vegetable" of all time. But don't let this French claim lead you to believe this tuber is native to France, or indeed that it has anything to do with the ancient city of Jerusalem, or that it is even an actual artichoke. Known as *Helianthus tuberosus* to botanists, but also called sunroot, sunchoke, earth apple or *topinambour,* it's officially a species of sunflower native to eastern North America. The so-called Jerusalem artichoke was eaten by various native tribes long before English and European settlers arrived, and as happened with other native staples, the newcomers needed food. According to one persuasive story, Italian immigrants first called the plant *girasole* (meaning sunflower), because of a visual similarity to the sunflower. In that way that languages often work among immigrats, the Italian word *girasole* sounded enough like "Jerusalem" to get swapped out over time. Another tale has the Pilgrims applying the name "Jerusalem artichoke" in honor of the New Jerusalem they were hoping to create in their little piece of the New World. The artichoke part of the name comes from the taste of its edible tuber. The notable explorer Samuel de Champlain sent the first samples of the plant back to France, remarking that its taste reminded him of artichokes. His enthusiasm explains the French involement with this intriguing plant.

TORTILLA ESPAÑOLA

2 tablespoons corn oil, divided

½ large onion, chopped

1 ½ cups crushed good-quality potato chips, preferably kettle style

6 eggs

½ teaspoon salt

¼ cup mascarpone cheese

5 slices jamon Serrano

2 canned pequillo peppers

A TORTILLA IN SPAIN IS A KIND OF FRITTATA—AN EGG DISH, NOT THE FAMILIAR THIN FLOUR OR CORN CIRCLE WE KNOW SO WELL. WE USE POTATO CHIPS INSTEAD OF THE CLASSIC CUBES OF FRIED POTATO, AND THE CHIPS SOAK UP EGG TO BECOME AN AMAZING SINGLE THING. WE LIKE TO SPLIT A SQUARE OF *TORTILLA ESPANOLA* IN HALF CROSSWAYS LIKE A BUN AND LOAD IT WITH CHEESE AND HAM LIKE A SANDWICH. IT'S PARTICULARLY GOOD WITH ITALIAN MORTADELLA.

Preheat the oven to 360° F. Heat ½ the oil in a small sauté pan and stir the onions until they are translucent, 5-7 minutes. Pour them into a stainless steel mixing bowl and combine with the potato chips, eggs and salt, forming a loose batter. Set the pan back over medium-low heat and pour in the batter, then transfer the pan to the oven until the tortilla is golden brown and cooked through, about 15 minutes. Remove from the heat.

When cool enough to handle safely, use a bread knife to slice the tortilla across like top and bottom hamburger buns and set the top aside. Spread the bottom with the mascarpone cheese then top with the ham and the peppers. Set the top back on. If desired, slice the round ends to form a square and slice into smaller squares. Serves 2 for lunch, or 4 as an appetizer.

POTATO

An Alsatian sculptor named Andreas Friederich erected a statue of Sir Francis Drake in southwest Germany in the 19th century, portraying the English explorer staring into the visionary horizon. His right hand rests on a sword, while his left grips a plant that many would recognize: a potato. The inscription on the base left nothing to guesswork: "Sir Francis Drake, *disseminator of the potato in Europe in the Year of Our Lord 1586. Millions of people who cultivate the earth bless his immortal memory.*" More than a few times the potato has been hailed as the most important food crop ever developed. And it all goes back to the Americas. To Peru. In their heyday high in the Andes, where the ruins of Machu Picchu remain their soaring testament, the Incas ate potatoes boiled, baked and mashed, as we do, but also boiled, peeled, chopped and dried to make *papas secas;* fermented in stagnant water to create sticky, odoriferous *toqosh;* and ground to pulp, soaked in a jug and filtered to produce *almidón de papa* (potato starch). Surely the most common preparation method was *chuño,* made by spreading potatoes outside to freeze on cold nights, then thawing them in the morning sun. Over several cycles of this, farmers squeezed out the water to produce a kind of ancient version of Italian gnocchi perfect for a spicy Andean stew. Even better, the stuff kept for years without refrigeration. Like the faro that kept Roman legions on the march, the potato kept Incan armies conquering all the land in sight of their high mountains. There are about five thousand potato varieties worldwide today, a full three thousand of them exclusive to the Andes—mainly in Peru, but also in Bolivia, Ecuador, Chile and Colombia.

BUFFALO CHILI WITH YUCA HASH

KNOWN INCORRECTLY FOR MORE THAN A CENTURY AS BUFFALO, BISON IS THE MOST AMERICAN OF MEATS. AND AT LEAST HERE IN TEXAS, WE BELIEVE THAT CHILI IS THAT MOST AMERICAN OF PREPARATIONS. COMBINE THOSE ELEMENTS WITH THE MEXICAN *MICHELADA*—A BLOODY MARY WITH BEER SERVED OVER YUCA, IT'S TRULY SOULFUL.

In a deep pan, sauté the bison with the pork butt until browned and starting to stick to pan. Stir in the onion, bell peppers and jalapeno, stirring to scrape browned bits from the pan. Cook until onion turns translucent. Add the beer, Bloody Mary mix and demi-glace, bringing to a boil to combine. Add all the dry spices, return to a boil, then reduce heat to simmer until liquid is reduced by ⅓, about 30 minutes.

Meanwhile, sauté the finely chopped boiled yuca in batches in a little butter and corn oil until golden brown, like hash brown potatoes. Keep warm. Fry the eggs in batches butter and corn oil, covering the pan with a lid for 2-3 minutes if you want "over easy" without flipping the eggs. Keep warm. On each appetizer plate, form a bed of yuca hash and top with bison chili. Top with diced onion, cilantro and panela cheese. Put a fried egg on top of each mound and serve immediately. Serves 12.

1 pound ground bison

¼ pound pork butt
(or prepared carnitas), diced

½ onion, diced

1 green bell pepper, diced

1 red bell pepper, diced

½ jalapeno, diced

1 (12-ounce) bottle Xingu
Brazilian beer

¾ cup Bloody Mary mix

1 ½ cup beef demi-glace
(see recipe p. 202)

2 tablespoons paprika

1 tablespoon ground cumin

2 teaspoons salt

1 teaspoon black pepper

1 teaspoon dried oregano

1 teaspoon garlic powder

½ teaspoon cayenne pepper

3 pounds boiled yuca,
finely chopped

12 eggs

Butter and corn oil for frying

½ onion, diced

¼ bunch fresh cilantro, chopped

2 cups grated panela cheese

BEEF EMPANADAS

½ cup raisins

3 tablespoons dry sherry

2 ¼ pound ground beef

1 bay leaf

½ teaspoon crushed red pepper

1 ½ teaspoon black pepper

1 ½ teaspoon smoked paprika

½ teaspoon ground cumin

2 tablespoons olive oil

2 ½ cups diced yellow onion

1 cup diced red bell pepper

½ cup chopped pimento-stuffed olives

¼ cup beef stock, concentrated

¾ cup dry (quick) oatmeal

Salt and pepper to taste

24 empanada pastry rounds, (choose ones for frying)

ALL OF OUR EMPANADAS USE THE SAME WRAPPER, WHICH CAN BE USED FOR EITHER BAKING OR FRYING. THE FILLING FOR OUR BEEF EMPANADAS IS PREPARED IN THE CLASSIC MANNER OF ARGENTINA, THE MEAT SEASONED GENEROUSLY WITH ONION, GARLIC AND CUMIN.

Soak the raisins in the sherry for 20 minutes. Meanwhile, in a large skillet, sauté the ground beef with the bay leaf in the olive oil until meat begins to brown and crumbly. Add onion and bell pepper, along with the red pepper, black pepper, paprika and cumin, cooking until vegetables are soft. Add the olives, raisins and concentrated beef stock, then stir in the oatmeal and cook until most liquid is absorbed, about 5 minutes. Season with salt and pepper. Discard bay leaf.

Spread the meat mixture onto a baking sheet and cool in refrigerator. Keeping your fingers damp with water, lay out the pastry circles and scoop about 3 tablespoons of the meat filling onto each, folding each into a half-moon and crimping the edges with a fork. Fry in oil preheated to 350° F until golden brown, about 4 minutes. Let cool a bit before eating. Makes 24 empanadas.

GUAVAS

The fruit known as guava is native to Mexico, Central America and the northern sections of South America, though they are now successfully cultivated and happily consumed all along the earth's tropical belt, including the Caribbean, Africa, South as well as Southeast Asia, Australia and New Zealand. In recent years, a significant guava crop has been launched in South Florida, along with many other tropical fruits. The term "guava" appears to derive from Arawak *guayabo*, clearly transported through the Spanish *guayaba*. It has been adapted into many European and Asian languages as some variation of the original. Another term, however, is *pera*, obviously derived from pear—a name the fruit carries around the Indian Ocean, thanks to Spanish and Portuguese explorers. To this day, Mexicans love the *agua fresca* made with guava, as well as guava-based sauces, desserts, candies and dried snack. *Pulque de guava* is a popular flavor of the native alcoholic drink. Because of its high degree of pectin, guava often finds its way into jellies, jams and marmalades across Latin America—treats known as *goiabada* in Brazil and as *bocadillo* in Venezuela and Colombia. Fresh slices of uncooked guava are beloved piece of street-food culture across the Americas, especially when the fruit is on ice and the weather is hot. Beyond their culinary popularity, guavas have been used for centuries in native remedies for a variety of ills—a tradition that has inspired tireless research beginning in the 1950s into its chemical identity. In preliminary lab research, extracts from guava leaves or bark have shown promise against cancer, bacterial infection, inflammation and pain.

CHICKEN EMPANADAS

AS WE MENTIONED, MY FAVORITE DISH AS A KID IN THE CHURRASCOS KITCHEN WAS *POLLO IN SALSA BLANCA,* CHICKEN COOKED IN A SHERRY CREAM SAUCE. SO IT'S NO SURPRISE THAT WHEN IT CAME TIME TO DEVELOP A CHICKEN EMPANADA, I HARKENED BACK TO SOME FAVORITE FLAVOR COMPONENTS, THEN ADDED THE TEXTURES OF BASIL, RED BELL PEPPER AND CANDIED PECANS.

Preheat oven to 300° F. To make the Chicken Thighs, lightly beat the egg whites in a large bowl with the Creole seasoning. Place the chicken in the bowl to coat thoroughly, then transfer them to a roasting pan. Roast for 20 minutes. Cool to room temperature. Cut meat from bones and shred using your fingers. You should have about 1 pound of chicken.

Make the Sherry Sauce. Cut the cold butter into cubes. Bring the sherry and concentrated chicken stock to a simmer in a pot over high heat. Simmer briefly until reduced and syrupy. Add cream and milk, bringing to a simmer while stirring constantly. Dissolve the cornstarch in the water and pour into the pot, reducing heat and letting sauce thicken. Add the cubes of butter a few at a time, whisking until melted and smooth. Strain through a fine sieve into a bowl and let cool.

In a pan, lightly sauté the onion and bell pepper in the oil until onion is transparent, about 5 minutes. Then add the shredded chicken and Sherry Sauce, bring to a simmer and cook 5 minutes. Turn off heat and add cheese. Spread filling over a sheet pan set in refrigerator to cool. On a lightly floured surface, set out the empanada disks and top each with a spoonful of filling. Top this with basil and candied pecan. Moisten the outer edge of each disk by touching with wet fingers, then fold into half moons enclosing the filling. Crimp the curved edge with the tines of a fork. Fry in oil preheated to 350° F until golden brown, about 4 minutes. Let cool a bit before eating. Makes 16 empanadas.

CHICKEN THIGHS

4 tablespoons egg whites

4 tablespoons Creole seasoning

2 pounds chicken thighs

SHERRY SAUCE

2 tablespoons butter, chilled

6 tablespoons dry sherry

3 tablespoons chicken stock, concentrated

3 cups heavy cream

2 cups milk

2 tablespoons cornstarch

2 tablespoons water

¾ cup diced yellow onion

5 tablespoons diced red bell pepper

¾ tablespoons corn oil

1 ¼ cup cotija cheese

16 empanada disks for frying

Thinly sliced basil leaves

Chopped candied pecans

SPINACH EMPANADAS

¼ baguette for crumbs
½ cup diced onion
½ tablespoon minced garlic
½ pound frozen spinach
¼ cup finely crumbled feta
8 empanada circles, for frying

ROCOTO SAUCE

1 ½ pound tomatoes
1 ½ pound red bell peppers
1 ½ cup rough chopped onion
3 tablespoons corn oil
8 cloves garlic
1 habanero pepper
¼ cup chopped rocoto pepper
(available frozen)
2 teaspoons salt

THE GUIDING LIGHT FOR THIS EMPANADA IS THE GREEK TRADITIONAL PHYLLO DISH *SPANAKOPITA*. INSTEAD OF PHYLLO, AN EMPANADA WRAPPER TAKES THE TERRIFIC SPINACH AND FETA FILLING. ROCOTO IS A PERUVIAN PEPPER SAUCE WHOSE SWEET HEAT IS REPLACED HERE BY CARAMELIZED ONION, TOMATO AND HABANERO.

Slice and toast the baguette till dry and crisp, then pulverize in a food processor to make ¼ cup of crumbs. Saute the onion and garlic in the oil. Purée the spinach and add it to the pan, stirring over medium-high heat to remove any water. Add the breadcrumbs and stir to incorporate. Turn off heat and stir in cheese. Season with the salt, if needed.

Using a 3-tablespoon ice cream scoop, place a ball of the spinach filling on each of the empanada circles, fold over to make a half-moon and crimp with a fork to seal rounded edges. Fry in oil preheated to 350° F for about 4 minutes or bake about 15 minutes until golden brown. Let cool before serving. Serve with Rocoto Sauce (see below). Makes 8.

ROCOTO SAUCE

Score the tomatoes by slicing a cross at one end and then drop into boiling water for a minute, until you see skins start to winkle and detach. On a grill or open flame, grill the red peppers for about 2 minutes, turning several times for coverage. Remove the skins from tomatoes and red peppers. Caramelize the onion in a large pan over medium-low heat, letting them turn golden. Add the peeled red peppers and garlic, cooking them gently without browning, about 15 minutes. When these vegetables are soft, add the tomato and rocoto pepper. Season with the salt. Purée until smooth in a food processor. Makes about 1 quart.

ANGEL WINGS

BLEU CHEESE SAUCE

4 ounces crumbled bleu cheese

2 tablespoons white vinegar

¼ cup water

1 cup good-quality mayonnaise

Peanut oil for frying

24 chicken wings

2 eggs

½ cup milk

2 cups all-purpose flour

6 tablespoons dry *caldo de pollo* granules

1 ½ tablespoon paprika

1 ½ teaspoon salt

⅓ cup butter

2 tablespoons Matouk West Indian hot sauce

AT THE FAMOUS HARRY'S BAR IN NEW YORK CITY, WE TASTED AN EXCITING SPINOFF OF THE TOO-FAMILIAR SPORTS-BAR WINGS. THIS DISH HAS FOUND CRAZY POPULARITY AT ARTISTA AND ON OUR CATERING MENUS. WE PARTICULARLY LOVE THE ADDITION OF MATOUK'S, A FIERY-SWEET SCOTCH BONNET AND PAPAYA PEPPER SAUCE FROM TRINIDAD AND TOBAGO, ROUNDED OUT BY BROWNED BUTTER.

To prepare the Bleu Cheese Sauce, combine the cheese, vinegar and water in a bowl, then fold in the mayonnaise until smooth.

In order to "French" the chicken wings, start with the middle joint—the one with the two parallel bones and the super-tender meat in between. Chop off both ends. Remove the skin and the larger of the two bones. Using your thumb and index finger, gently push all the meat to one end, forming a ball or knob.

Make an egg wash by beating the eggs with the milk. In a separate bowl, make seasoned flour by combining the flour, *caldo de pollo* granules, paprika and salt. Dip the meat end of each wing into the egg wash and then dredge in the seasoned flour, covering completely. Deep fry the wings in peanut oil at 350° F until golden, about 8 minutes.

Melt the butter in a saucepan while whisking. Cook until it browns, releasing a nutty, toasty or "bread-y" aroma. Strain through fine mesh and let cool slightly. Stir in the Matouk's hot sauce. Transfer Angel Wings to a platter and drizzle with the browned butter glaze. Serve with a bowl of the Bleu Cheese Sauce for dipping. Makes 24 wings.

DUCK CONFIT PUPUSAS

IN HOUSTON, OUR CHURCH SERVES PUPUSAS AFTER MASS. IF WE WEREN'T GOING ALREADY, THAT WOULD BE REASON ENOUGH TO ATTEND. WHILE SIMILAR TO THE *AREPAS* SERVED IN PARTS OF SOUTH AMERICA, PUPUSAS ARE A UNIQUE SALVADORAN SPECIALTY BUILT AROUND THICK LAYERS OF *MASA* WITH A FILLING OF PORK AND CHEESE. WE WERE CURIOUS TO DISCOVER IF THERE WAS A WAY TO MAKE THE ORIGINAL BETTER, AND WE DISCOVERED SEVERAL—INCLUDING TOPPING THE WHOLE THING WITH FRENCH DUCK CONFIT (NOW AVAILABLE IN GOURMET MARKETS) AND FRYING UP THE DUCK SKINS TO MAKE *CHICHARRONES*.

1 cup julienned white cabbage

1 cup julienned carrots

1 cup pickled onions

2 cups prepared duck confit with skin

3 cups masa harina

1 ½ teaspoon kosher salt

2 ¼ cup warm water

1 cup queso fresco

2 cups mozzarella cheese

1 ½ cup refried black beans

Preheat oven to 200° F. In a bowl, combine the cabbage, carrots and pickled onions to form a slaw, letting the vegetables marinate until ready to use. Remove the skin from the duck confit and place in the oven for 45 minutes to dehydrate, then fry in 350° F corn oil until frisp. In a large bowl, mix the masa harina, salt and warm water together using your hands. Add the queso fresco. Cover and refrigerate for 15 minutes. Make the filling in a food processor by thoroughly incorporating the mozzarella, refried beans and fried duck skin.

Tear off 1 ½ tablespoon balls of the dough and roll out on a clean, floured surface to about 2-inch circles. Lay the circles onto the bottom of tart pans lined with plastic wrap and top each with about 1 tablespoon of the filling. Top each with another circle of dough and press gently to seal. Cook the pupusas until golden brown in a nonstick pan with cooking spray, about 3 minutes per side. Top each warm pupusa with about 3 tablespoons on the confit and then with the cabbage slaw. Makes about 24 pupusa.

PICA PIEDRAS

1 (3-4-pound) rack of baby back pork ribs

15 thin slices bacon (preferable "wide-shingled")

Water

4 cloves garlic

2 tablespoons chopped ginger

1 cup agave nectar

¼ cup soy sauce

¼ cup tamarind paste (such as Thai Panda)

THE VERY FIRST TIME WE LAID EYES ON THIS EXTRA-LARGE SLAB OF PORK RIBS, WE REMEMBERED THE RACK OF DINOSAUR MEAT THAT TIPPED OVER FRED FLINTSTONE'S CAR IN THE OLD CARTOON SERIES. THIS IS ACTUALLY THE FIRST DISH MY DAD AND I WORKED ON TOGETHER AFTER I MOVED HOME TO HOUSTON FROM CALIFORNIA. IT WAS OUR WAY OF WORKING OUT A PORK VERSION OF OUR CHICKEN ANGEL WINGS. WE'RE ESPECIALLY FOND OF WORKING IN THE TAMARIND, USED ALL ALONG THE EQUATOR FROM ASIA TO THE AMERICAS. THEIR SWEET-SOUR QUALITY ADDS SO MUCH TO PORK.

Preheat oven to 275° F. Cut and pull away the silver skin from the back side of the ribs. Cut into individual ribs, about 15. Starting on the "spine side" with looser, more separate ribs, use a sharp knife to carefully slice all meat from the bone, essentially peeling it back and down. When almost to the far end, user your hands to firmly gather and press the meat into a ball or know with the bone as the "handle" for eating. Wrap each ball of meat in a strip of bacon.

Stand the ribs on a baking pan with a grill grate inside. Pour some water into the pan to create steam. Add the garlic and ginger to the water for flavor and aroma. Set pan in oven for 3 hours. As the cooking nears its end, combine the agave nectar, soy and tamarind paste. Use this to coat the meat as it finishes cooking. Remove from heat and drizzle with additional glaze. Serves 6.

ALLSPICE

Allspice takes its name because it tastes like the beloved dessert trio of cinnamon, nutmeg and mace. But Jamaicans, who grow most of the world's supply, don't call it that. From Negril to Port Antonio to Kingston, cooks know the spice as pimento, setting up confusion in the Spanish-speaking world. Allspice is the only spice grown exclusively in the Western Hemisphere, an evergreen tree that produces its berries and is indigenous to the rainforests of South and Central America. Today, while Jamaica dominates the world market, other sources include Guatemala, Honduras and Mexico. Jamaican allspice is considered to be superior due to its higher oil content. Allspice was imported to Europe soon after the discovery of the New World. There were attempts to transplant it to regions of the Far East, but those trees produced little fruit. The English, who ruled Jamaica for most of its existence, started regular shipments home in 1737, but its export became overshadowed by such other New World products as sugar and coffee. Allspice did find an audience in England eventually, coming to be known as English spice.

PROSCIUTTO AND MASCARPONE PUFFS

4 tablespoons butter

1 cup water

1 tablespoon sugar

1 teaspoon salt

1 cup all-purpose flour

4 plus 2 eggs

¼ cup milk

1 cup mascarpone cheese, at room temperature

1 pound Serrano ham or prosciutto, sliced paper-thin

½ cup honey

1 teaspoon aji amarillo paste

THE NAME MEANS "ÉCLAIR" IN SPANISH, BUT THESE ARE SAVORY. I FIRST ENCOUNTERED THE BASIC IDEA WHILE BACKPACKING THROUGH ITALY. A SIMPLE, SMALL TRATTORIA BROUGHT OUT FRIED BREAD FILLED WITH MASCARPONE THAT HAD BEEN WRAPPED IN PROSCIUTTO AND DRIZZLED WITH HONEY.

Preheat the oven to 425° F. Melt the butter in the water over medium-high heat. When just boiling, dissolve the sugar and salt in the water and bring back to a boil. Add the flour all at once, still over heat, and stir for 3-4 minutes until the batter is the consistency of mashed potatoes, with no lumps of unmixed flour. Transfer the batter to a mixer with a leaf attachment. Turn slowly as the batter cools slightly.

One at a time, break the 4 eggs into the mixing bowl and give each time to incorporate with the batter, slowing the mixture for each addition and then speeding it up again. Stop occasionally and scrap down the sides of the bowl. You need to mix until batter is "wavy"—that is, until it waves or shimmies when you shake it gently hanging from the leaf attachment or from a spoon.

Spoon batter into a pastry bag and pipe circles of about 1 tablespoon each onto a baking sheet lined with parchment paper. Make egg wash by beating the 2 eggs with the milk in a bowl. Brush each circle with the egg wash. Bake for 8 minutes, then lower oven temperature to 375° F and bake until golden and puffy, about 10 minutes more.

Let puffs cool slightly. Cut the ham into long slices. Fill a pastry bag with mascarpone. Using a paring knife, poke a hole in the bottom of each puff and pipe in mascarpone. Wrap each puff in two slices of ham, wrapping them across each other. Seal with a toothpick, if desired. In a small mixing bowl, combine the honey and aji Amarillo paste and drizzle over the tops of the relampagos. Makes about 40.

BEEF BRISKET FLAUTAS

WE MARRIED THIS TEX-MEX FAVORITE WITH TEXAS BEEF BARBECUE FOR OUR FAMILY-FRIENDLY AMAZÓN GRILL. IF YOU SMOKE YOUR OWN BRISKET AT HOME, THIS IS A GREAT WAY TO EXTEND WHATEVER MEAT IS LEFT AFTER THE FIRST ASSAULT. AND IF YOU DON'T, A GROWING NUMBER OF STORES IN TEXAS OFFER BRISKET THAT'S ALREADY SMOKED. FLAUTA IS SPANISH FOR "FLUTE," WE GRILL OURS BEFORE FRYING FOR ADDED CHAR FLAVOR.

Shred meat with fork. In a sauté pan, sauté the onion, peppers and garlic in olive oil. Add the shredded brisket and the cheese. Holding with tongs, dip each corn tortilla in hot oil then pass it carefully over a gas flame to char and make pliable. Roll the tortillas tightly around the filling and fry in oil preheated to 350° F until golden brown, 3-4 minutes. Makes 16 flautas. Serve hot with Cranberry Chutney for dipping.

CRANBERRY CHUTNEY

Sauté the apple and shallot in the butter until translucent, then add the fresh ginger, ground ginger, cinnamon and crushed red pepper. Stir to incorporate. Add the cranberry sauce and heat to liquify. Transfer to a bowl.

2 pounds smoked beef brisket, trimmed of fat

1 cup chopped onion

1 cup chopped red bell pepper

1 cup chopped Serrano pepper

3 tablespoons minced garlic

1 tablespoon olive oil

2 cups shredded smoked panela cheese

16 enchilada-sized corn tortillas

CRANBERRY CHUTNEY

1 red apple, diced

1 shallot, diced

1 tablespoon unsalted butter

1 tablespoon minced fresh ginger

⅛ teaspoon ground ginger

⅛ teaspoon ground cinnamon

⅛ teaspoon crushed red pepper

1 can prepared cranberry sauce

PAPAYA

People tend to think of papaya as being tropical, the stuff of island vacation dreams. The exotically orange fruit probably did originate in the wild along the Caribbean coast of Central America. Scholars say it was widely cultivated by Indians in Mexico and Central America long before the arrival of Columbus in 1492. The navigator contributed to papaya legend when he sampled a slice and declared it the "fruit of the angels." These early papaya purveyors called the fruit *ambapaya*, which clearly had an impact on the great botanical namer, Linnaeus. He gave the fruit the name *Carica papaya* in 1753, and over the centuries the second half of the Latin name stuck. There are about thirty different species of papaya, most so similar that few would notice any variation. During the 16th and 17th centuries, papaya quickly became a favorite of Spanish and Portuguese explorers. Together they spread papaya love and indeed the plant itself from tropical America to nearby islands in the Caribbean, and from there to the Pacific and Southeast Asia. This process was made easier because papaya seeds, once dried, can be planted successfully for several years. Finally, in the 20th century, papayas were brought to the United States and have been cultivated in Hawaii, the major domestic producer since the 1920s. In England the fruit has often been called pawpaw, though in the United States that causes confusion with another pawpaw, the very different *Asimina triloba*.

FULL
Plates

We got our start grilling steaks.

Though we still love our churrascos as much as we did when they inspired our
first restaurant, we've traveled a long road of discovery in terms of entrées.
Seafood has become a major fascination for our customers here in Texas.
America's embrace of sushi, sashimi, ceviche and crudi, essentially give us
permission to cook fish the way it tastes best, rather than cooking it to death
the way most places had to do in the old days. In the quarter-century we've
spent inviting guests into our restaurants that we hope feel like our home,
we've seen and responded to many changes in taste, many trends and more
than a few fads. Sometimes we'll experiment with a fad, but we never allow
ourselves to wander far or long from the mantra: Latin, artistic and yummy.

PARGO AMÉRICAS

CREMA

4 cups heavy cream

½ cup sour cream

1 tablespoon cornstarch

1 tablespoon water

2 teaspoons salt

8 ears yellow corn, shucked

Creole seasoning

1 cup Egg White Marinade
(see p. 203)

6 eggs

2 cups milk

2 cups all-purpose flour

½ cup cotija cheese,
plus additional

6 (8-ounce) snapper fillets

¼ cup corn oil

Achiote oil

2-3 fresh limes

THIS DISH BUILT ON SNAPPER, THE KING OF ALL GULF FISH, WAS INSPIRED BY THE CHARGRILLED CORN SOLD BY STREET VENDORS ALL OVER MEXICO. ALL OF THE BASIC FLAVORS ARE THERE ON THE STREET—CREAM, LIME JUICE, SPICES AND QUESO FRESCO, AS THOUGH JUST WAITING FOR US TO TURN THEM INTO A CRUST FOR SNAPPER. IT'S FINISHED WITH THE TRADITIONAL GRILLED CORN ACCOMPANIMENTS OF MEXICAN CREAM AND SPICY SEASONAL.

To make the Crema, combine the heavy cream with the sour cream in a pot and bring just to a boil. Dissolve the cornstarch in the water and add it to the creams to thicken. Season with salt. Keep the crema warm.

To prepare the fish, thoroughly char the ears of corn on a grill. Cut the kernels off the corn to yield about 4 cups. Make sure the kernels are dry. In a bowl, season the snapper fillets with Creole seasoning and pour on the egg white marinade, thoroughly coating each fillet. In a bowl, whisk the eggs and then whisk in the milk until incorporated. Set up three bowls: the egg mixture closest the fish, then a bowl with the flower and then a pan with the corn kernels mixed with the cotija.

Preheat the broiler. In a process, dip one side of each snapper fillet in the egg mixture, then in the flour, then back in the egg mixture, then back in the flour—double coating, but only on one side. Press the coated side down onto the corn, making the kernels adhere. Sear the fish in a pan coated in a little corn oil in batches of 1 or 2 fillets. Flip the fish carefully onto a baking sheet, corn side up. When ready, set under the broiler until fish is cooked through, about 8 minutes. Set the fish atop a pool of crema drizzled with achiote oil for color. Squeeze lime over the top of the fish. Serves 6.

SWORDFISH CHURRASCO

SPINACH QUINOTTO

1 ½ cups cooked quinoa

1 ½ cups blanched and chopped spinach

¾ cup vegetable stock

¾ cup Crema America (see recipe p. 116)

¾ cup grated Parmesan cheese

4 Roma tomatoes, seeded

6 tablespoons thinly sliced basil leaves

4 tablespoons olive oil

Salt and pepper

6 (8-ounce) swordfish loin steaks

Kosher Salt

¾ cup Chimichurri (see recipe p. 140)

12 (U-12) shrimp, peeled

⅓ cup Achiote Marinade (see recipe p. 128)

Habanero Beurre Blanc, warm (see recipe p. 128)

THE STEAK LIKE QUALITY OF SWORDFISH LENDS ITSELF SO WELL TO THE CHURRASCO TREATMENT. THE LOIN IS UNROLLED IN THE SAME WAY AS BEEF TENDERLOIN, BASTED IN CHIMICHURRI AND CHAR GRILLED. IT HAS THE ADDED COMPONENT OF A TOMATO TOPPING REMINISCENT OF ITALIAN BRUSCHETTA.

Prepare the Spinach Quinotto by combining the cooked quinoa, spinach and vegetable stock in a pan over medium-high heat. Bring the mixture to a boil and allow liquid to reduce as quinoa absorbs stock, 3-4 minutes. Add the Parmesan and Crema, tossing to incorporate. Keep warm.

Prepare the topping for the swordfish (similar to traditional tomato bruschetta topping in Italy). Combine the tomato, basil and olive oil in a bowl, tossing until coated. Season to taste with salt and pepper.

Season the swordfish steaks with salt and brush with Chimichurri. Toss the shrimp with the Achiote Marinade. Grill the shrimp over a hot fire just until cooked through, 4-6 minutes. Grill the swordfish about 1 minute on the presentation side to form grill marks, then turn it to form grill marks on the other side. Be careful not to overcook fish. Transfer grilled swordfish to a plate along with Spinach Quinotto. Top fish with tomato-basil mixture and with Habanero Beurre Blanc. Serves 6.

PAELLA

PAELLA IS ALL ABOUT THE RICE. OUR VALENCIA STYLE RICE DISH IS DEEPLY AROMATIC USING SPANISH CHORIZO, SAFFRON AND SHRIMP STOCK. IN A PARTY SETTING, WE LOVE TO CREATE A PAELLA STATION WITH SEVERAL VARIETIES OF SEAFOOD, SO PEOPLE CAN CHOOSE THE TYPE THEY LOVE BEST.

Heat the oil in a large pot. Brown the chorizo in the oil. Stir in paprika, saffron and crushed red pepper to achieve a bright reddish yellow color. Stir for 1-2 minutes, then add the onions, peppers and garlic. Stir until onions are golden and transparent. Add the rice and stir to fry for 2-3 minutes. Dilute the chicken stock concentrate in the water and add to the pot, followed by the shrimp stock and the wine.

Cook the rice traditionally, bringing to a boil, lowering heat and covering until the liquid is absorbed about 20 minutes. Or, for even better results, boil the rice in the liquid uncovered for about 20 minutes, until liquid first foams on top as it evaporates and finally small caverns open up. Do not stir until the liquid is gone. Remove the pot from heat, cover with foil and let sit for 20 minutes. Stir and serve with the grilled seafood of your choice. Serves 10-12.

1 tablespoon olive oil
½ pound Spanish chorizo, sliced
1 tablespoon Spanish smoked paprika
1 teaspoon saffron threads
½ teaspoon crushed red pepper
1 ½ cup chopped onion
1 ½ cup chopped green bell pepper
1 ½ cup chopped red bell pepper
1 tablespoon minced garlic
4 cups par boiled rice
3 tablespoon chicken stock, concentrated
4 cups water
4 cups shrimp broth
½ cup dry white wine

ZUCCHINI
In a sense, the summer squash known by the Italian name zucchini is a product of the New World that seems new all over again. As few as three decades ago in the United States, home cooks knew little about it. And as with so many other gifts of the Americas to the world, they credited its development to Italy. *Cucurbita pepo* is a member of the cucumber and melon family enjoyed by inhabitants of Central and South America for several thousand years. Christopher Columbus originally brought seeds to the Mediterranean region and Africa. And somewhere along that long road, the name attached itself. The word *zucchini* comes from the Italian *zucchino,* meaning a small squash. The term *squash* comes from the Indian *skutasquash* meaning "green thing eaten green," which zucchini undeniably are. The alternative name *courgette* is from the French word for squash (*courge*), with the same spelling, and is commonly used in France, Ireland and the United Kingdom. In South Africa, interestingly, zucchini are known as baby marrow. After going largely unknown for a long time, zucchini are a beloved vegetable (or an immature fruit, to be precise), turning up in all sorts of vegetable dishes, as well as in breads and even desserts.

POLLO ENCAMISADO

TEMPURA BATTER

2 cups all-purpose flour

1 ½ cups cornstarch

1 ½ tablespoon salt

1 tablespoon baking powder

2 cups cold water

1 cup crushed ice

PLANTAIN CRUST

3 cups broken-up plantain chips

1 cup Japanese Panko breadcrumbs

1 teaspoon powdered caldo de pollo

⅓ cup grated smoked cotija cheese

1 teaspoon salt

1 teaspoon powdered sugar

BLACK BEAN SAUCE

3 strips bacon

1 stick unsalted butter

1 yellow onion, chopped

1 can refried black beans

1 tablespoon Worcestershire sauce

Salt to taste

8 (4-ounce) chicken breast halves

2 Roma tomatoes, blanched, peeled and quartered

Smoked panela cheese, sliced ¼-inch thick

WHAT A WONDERFUL NAME: "CHICKEN IN A SHIRT." IN THIS CASE, THE "SHIRT" IS FORMED OF OUR SIGNATURE PLANTAIN CHIPS. WHAT WE END UP WITH, AND WHY WE THINK IT'S SO DELICIOUS, IS A KIND OF LATINIZED CHICKEN PARMESAN—COMPLETE WITH OUR SPICY BLACK BEAN SAUCE, ROASTED TOMATO AND SMOKED AND SEARED PANELA CHEESE. THE MILD SWEETNESS IN THE PLANTAIN COMPLEMENTS SPICY BLACK BEAN.

Make the tempura batter by combining all the dry ingredients in a large bowl and whisking in cold water and ice. Keep the smooth batter chilled until ready to use. Make the plantain crust by pulsing the chips until uniformly crumbled but not reduced to powder. Combine with all remaining crust ingredients.

Make the black bean sauce by chopping up the bacon and cooking in a pan until crisp. Add the butter and sauté the onion until golden brown. Add the refried beans, seasoning with Worcestershire sauce and salt. After 15-20 minutes to let flavors meld, let mixture cool enough to place in food processor or blender. Purée until smooth. Return to pan and keep warm.

Sear the tomato quarters and panela squares in a hot pan. Pound out the chicken breasts to achieve a uniform thickness. Heat a fryer to 350° F. Dredge each breast in the tempura batter and then crust generously with the plantain mixture. Fry the breasts until golden brown, 5-7 minutes. Spoon black bean sauce onto 4 dinner plates and top with the chicken breasts. Top each with tomato and panela. Serves 4-6.

ARROZ CON POLLO NUEVO

4 chicken thighs, skin on
1 cup rice
½ cup chopped onion
2 cups chicken stock

WHEN I'M COOKING AT HOME, I FREQUENTLY MAKE THIS SIMPLE, YUMMY SPIN OF THE TRADITIONAL LATIN "RICE WITH CHICKEN." I LOVE CHICKEN THIGHS, SINCE THEY HAVE MORE FLAVOR AND STAY MOISTER IN COOKING THAN THE NOW-OMNIPRESENT CHICKEN BREAST. I ALSO LOVE TO CRISP THE SKIN IN THE OVEN AND SERVE IT ON THE SIDE OF THE PLATE. IT'S A GREAT DECORATION, EXCEPT AROUND OUR FAMILY IT DISAPPEARS VERY QUICKLY.

Preheat oven to 350° F. Set the chicken pieces skin side-up in a pan and roast for 1 hour. Let cool enough to handle. Carefully remove the skin from each thigh in one piece. Pour the fat and other liquid from the roasting pan into a sauté pan and use this to sauté the onion for 3-4 minutes over medium-high heat. Pour in the rice and stir until it starts to turn golden brown. Add the chicken stock, cover and reduce heat. Cook until all liquid is absorbed and rice is tender, about 20 minutes.

Remove the thighs from the pan and remove all meat, shredding with your fingers into bite-sized pieces. Return the chicken skin to the pan and set in oven, letting it get crisp in the heat. When the rice is cooked, stir in the boneless chicken. Transfer chicken-rice mixture to a plate or platter and decorate with strips of crispy chicken skin. Serves 4-6.

TURKEY

The birds we call turkeys are native to the Americas (North America, mostly, with a related appearance in Mexico's Yucatan Peninsula which includes all or part of the states of Quintana Roo, Campeche, Yucatan, Tabasco and Chiapas, along with sections of Belize and Guatemala. Turkeys were so American, in fact, that they were considered for "national bird" honor, losing out to the American Bald Eagle. Benjamin Franklin thought the eagle too bloodthirsty, making the peace-loving turkey a better choice for the newborn nation. When Europeans first encountered turkeys in the Americas, they incorrectly identified the birds as a type of guineafowl (*Numididae*) that were also known as turkey fowl (or turkey hen and turkey cock) because they were imported through the country Turkey. Shortened to just the name of the country, the identification stuck. In 1550, an English navigator named William Strickland, who had introduced the turkey into England, was granted a coat of arms including a *"turkey-cock in his pride proper."* In addition to this simple mistake, there was a genuine belief that the newly discovered Americas were in fact part of Asia, plus a tendency to attribute exotic animals and foods to exotic lands.

ACHIOTE TURKEY BREAST

THIS HAS BEEN A HOLIDAY STAPLE OF OURS WITH ACHIOTE, TYPICALLY RESERVED FOR PORK, BRINGING EXCITEMENT TO THE HOLIDAY TABLE. THE TECHNIQUE OF WRAPPING AND TYING TWO TURKEY BREASTS IN THE SKIN ASSURES MOISTURE AND EVEN COOKING.

If skin remains attached to the turkey breast halves, remove it carefully so it doesn't tear. Press the halves together, thick end meeting thin end, forming a uniform thickness of meat. Wrap the skin around about ½ the turkey and tie with kitchen twine. Sprinkle with salt and allow to air cure in the refrigerator for 12 hours.

When ready to cook, melt the butter in a large saucepan and carefully (it will splatter) add all remaining ingredients. Brush this achiote basting liquid all over the turkey skin and place skin side over indirect heat on a grill preheated to medium-high. Cook for 30 minutes, then turn the other side down. Cook for an additional 45 minutes, basting occasionally, until a meat thermometer registers 165° F in the thickest portion of the breast. Slice and serve. Serves 8-10.

2 turkey breast halves, purchased with skin

Salt

2 cups clarified butter

½ cup orange juice

⅓ cup lemon juice

3 tablespoons lime juice

2 tablespoons white wine vinegar

½ teaspoon ground cumin

7 ½ ounces achiote (annatto) paste

½ teaspoon dried oregano

½ teaspoon kosher salt

ACHIOTE (ANNATTO)

Though known in Latin as *Bixa orellana* and often sold around the world as annatto, achiote is a New World plant. In the paste form, favored in Yucatán, Oaxacan, and Belizean cuisine, it's made from slightly bitter, earthy flavored red seeds, mixed with other spices and ground. Achiote is a distinctly colored red-yellow-orange. It originates as a shrub or small tree originating in the tropical region of the Americas, and derives its name from the Nahuatl word *āchiotl*. It's also known as *aploppas,* and by its original Tupi name *urucu.* The Spanish found it growing in the Americas and introduced it to Southeast Asia in the 17th century. Achiote is best known as the source of the natural pigment annatto, used as a colorant and condiment for traditional dishes of the Americas such as *cochinita pibil,* chicken in achiote and *caldo de olla.* It is used to add color to butter, cheese, popcorn, drinks and breads, and it is a key ingredient in the drink *tascalate* that's popular in the Mexican state of Chiapas. The main achiote growers can be found in Bolivia, Brazil, Colombia, Ecuador, India, Jamaica, Mexico, Peru, Puerto Rico and the Dominican Republic.

CERDO RELLENO

CILANTRO TAMALES

2 ½ cups pre-cooked arepa meal

1 cup crumbled panela cheese

1 cup grated cotija cheese

½ cup cilantro

1 teaspoon chopped garlic

1 jalapeno, stem and seeds removed

2 ½ cups water

¼ cup white wine vinegar

1 teaspoon salt

ACHIOTE MARINADE

½ cup orange juice

⅓ cup lemon juice

3 tablespoons lime juice

2 tablespoons white wine vinegar

½ teaspoon ground cumin

7 ½ ounces achiote (annatto) paste

½ teaspoon dried oregano

½ teaspoon kosher salt

2 cups corn oil

HABANERO BEURRE BLANC

1 habanero

3 cloves garlic

3 tablespoons lime juice

3 tablespoons white wine vinegar

½ cup heavy cream

¼ cup sour cream

½ teaspoon cornstarch

½ teaspoon water

1 pound butter, chilled

4 pork tenderloins,
cut into 2 halves

THIS DISH STARTED OUT SIMPLY AS A "PORK TAMALE TURNED INSIDE OUT," WITH THE MASA ON THE INSIDE AND THE PORK ON THE OUTSIDE, THE WHOLE THING STEAMED IN CORN HUSKS AND SEASONED WITH ACHIOTE.

To prepare the Cilantro Tamales, mix the arepa meal and cheese together in a large bowl. Purée all remaining ingredients together in a food processor to produce a bright green liquid, then pour this into the dry ingredients. Knead this dough with your hands until thoroughly incorporated and set in refrigerator for 30 minutes. At that time, form the dough into logs about ¾ inch thick and 4 inches long. You should end up with 8 logs. On a pan, set in the freezer for at least 3-4 hours to harden.

Make the Achiote Marinade by placing all ingredients in a blender and puréeing until smooth. Pour into a bowl or other container. Rinse out the blender and prepare the Habanero Beurre Blanc. Purée in habanero, garlic, lime juice and vinegar. In a sauce-pan, heat the cream with the sour cream to a simmer. Make a slurry by dissolving the cornstarch in the water and add this to the mixture, bringing just to a boil to thicken. Reduce heat to low and add in the butter very slowly, whisking until each addition is melted and smooth. Finish with 1 ½ teaspoons of the habanero-garlic purée, reserving the rest for spicing anything. Makes about 2 cups.

To complete the dish, take the pork tenderloin halves and insert a long, narrow knife in one end till it comes out the other, then repeat from the opposite side. Slice carefully to open up the center, then use your fingers to promote a cavity wide enough to hold a tamale. Retrieve the tamales from the freezer and insert one into each tenderloin serving. Cover each tenderloin with about 1 tablespoon of the Achiote Marinade, using your hands to cover completely.

Wrap each serving of Cerdo Relleno in a tamale husk that's been soaked in hot water for 3 minutes, then seal it inside aluminum foil with the ends folded in. Placing each seam-side down, set the rellenos in a steamer over medium high heat. Seal the steam with aluminum foil and cook until pork's internal temperature is above 140, about 20 minutes.

Let rest in foil for 10 more minutes, to let cooking continue and reach about medium.

To serve, unwrap rellenos from foil and husk. Slice into 2 halves, or perhaps into 4 medallions, and serve hot, with warm Habanero Beurre Blanc drizzled over the top. Serves 8.

CARNITAS PIBÍL

CARNITAS

5 pounds pork butt

1 ½ tablespoons Creole seasoning

¼ cup Achiote Marinade (see recipe p. 128)

1 ½ cups milk

1 cup Coca-Cola

GUAJILLO SAUCE

1 cup crushed guajillo chile

1 cup crushed ancho chile

¼ cup dried chipotle chile

¾ cup peeled garlic cloves

1 cinnamon stick

5 cups boiling water

1 ½ teaspoons oregano

1 teaspoon black pepper

3 whole cloves

½ teaspoon ground cumin

3 tablespoons honey

3 cups chicken stock

⅓ cup corn oil

DEEP-FRIED YUCA CAKES

3 pounds peeled yuca

1 ½ gallons water

¼ cup plus 1 teaspoon salt

3 tablespoons cotija cheese

PIBIL IS THE YUCATAN VERSION OF THE HAWAIIAN LUAUA TRADITION, IN WHICH A PIG IS BURIED IN THE GROUND WITH HOT COALS. SINCE LATIN AMERICA ISN'T TRADITIONALLY WINE-CENTRIC, WE WILL OFTEN BRAISE MEATS IN A MIXTURE INVOLVING THE EVER-PRESENT COCA-COLA. IN ADDITION TO IRRESISTIBLY TENDER PORK, THERE'S THE TASTE OF GUAJILLO PEPPERS, CITRUS AND RED ONION.

To cook the Carnitas, cut the pork butt into 2-inch cubes. In a mixing bowl, season the pork with the Creole seasoning, then cover with the Achiote Marinade. Marinate for at least 1 hour—overnight is better—in the refrigerator. Preheat oven to 325º F. Transfer the pork to a roasting pan. Pour in the milk and Coca-Cola. Cover the pan tightly with aluminum foil and place in the oven, checking occasionally until meat is tender, about 4 hours.

Prepare the Guajillo Sauce by toasting the chiles, garlic cloves and cinnamon stick in a dry pan until browned and blistered, pressing down chiles as they soften. Pour the mixture into a large container and add the boiling water, letting it steep like tea for 10 minutes. Strain and discard the water. Place the browned chile mixture and the oregano, black pepper, whole cloves, cumin, honey and chicken stock in a blender and purée until smooth. Heat the corn oil in a pan and, being careful not to splatter, pour the purée into the pan. Stir to incorporate the oil and cook about 5 minutes over medium-high heat.

To make the Cakes, boil the yuca in water with ½ cup salt until tender. Let yuca cool, then grate using either the grater attachment on a food processor or a cheese grater. In a mixing bowl, combine with the cotija and 1 teaspoon salt. Using your hands, form this dough into 10-12 cakes about ½ inch thick and drop into a deep fryer preheated to 350º F, until golden brown. To serve, set a yuca cake at the center of each dinner plate and top with chunks of Carnitas. Spoon sauce over the top and around the plate. Serves 10-12.

KOREAN FRIED QUAIL

HOUSTON HAS ALL KINDS OF ASIAN FOOD, INCLUDING WONDERFUL KOREAN RESTAURANTS NOW TOPPED IN MANY OF OUR MINDS BY KOREAN. ONE OF OUR FAVORITE THINGS IS THE WAY THEY TWICE-FRY CHICKEN TO PRODUCE AN EXTRA-CRISPY CRUST AND THEN DRIZZLE ON A SWEET-HEAT GLAZE. THIS IS OUR HOMAGE TO THAT CHICKEN, REDIRECTED TO FLAVORFUL TEXAS QUAIL.

Prepare the Glaze by whisking the ingredients together in a mixing bowl. To make the seasoned flour, mix all ingredients except the quail and egg wash together in a separate bowl. Dredge each quail in the seasoned flour, then in the egg wash and then back in the flour until thoroughly coated. Deep-fry the quail in corn oil heated to 350° F for 4 minutes. Remove the quail from the oil and drain on paper towels. Return the quail to the hot oil and fry until golden brown, another 4 minutes. Drain again on paper towels, then spoon the glaze over the top of each fried bird. Serves 8.

GLAZE

⅔ cup ketchup

⅔ cup rice vinegar

½ cup Korean pepper paste

8 cloves garlic, minced

½ cup all-purpose flour

½ cup rice flour

1 cup potato starch

1 tablespoon powdered chicken bouillon

1 tablespoon garlic powder

1 teaspoon baking soda

1 teaspoon salt

1 teaspoon black pepper

1 teaspoon paprika

1 teaspoon onion powder

½ teaspoon ground red pepper

8 semi-boneless quail

1 cup egg wash
(see recipe p. 203)

Corn oil for deep frying

VIGORÓN

½ cup white vinegar

2 tablespoons malt vinegar

¼ cup water

2 teaspoons sugar

1 ½ teaspoons salt

¼ teaspoon crushed red pepper

¼ teaspoon black pepper

4 ½ cups shredded cabbage

¼ cup finely sliced yellow onion

⅓ cup finely sliced green
bell pepper

⅓ cup diced Roma tomato

2 pounds peeled yuca

1 gallon water

Salt

5 cups chopped Carnitas Pibil
(see recipe p. 130)

THIS IS A GREAT NICARAGUAN STREET FOOD, THE KIND OF THING WORKERS FROM OF-
FICE TO FACTORY TURN TO FOR "SECOND BREAKFAST" ABOUT TEN IN THE MORNING.
YOU GET THE LAYERS OF YUCA, FRIED PORK AND CABBAGE SLAW HANDED TO YOU IN A
PLANTAIN LEAF. NO FORK, KNIFE OR SPOON REQUIRED. AND THE PLATE IS DEFINITELY
BIODEGRADABLE.

In a bowl, combine the vinegars, water, sugar, salt and spices. Add the cabbage, onion,
bell, pepper and tomato. Cover bowl and let marinate for at least 2 hours. Meanwhile,
boil the peeled yuca until tender in salted water. Drain. To serve, divide boiled yuca over
dinner plates and top with chunks of Carnitas Pibil. Spoon the pickled cabbage over the
top of the meat. Serves 6-8.

YUCA

Beginning its life as early as 10,000 B.C. as a wild plant in southwest Brazil and Paraguay, the important and nourishing fruit (also known around
the New World as cassava) eventually spread by pollen as far north as the Gulf of Mexico. It was here that the Maya made the most serious
and successful efforts at cultivation, making it before long one of the cornerstones of their diet. The fact that cassava is also known as manioc
(indeed its Latin name comes down to us as *manihot esculenta*) is the result of a strange legend from the Tupi culture about a young woman
named Mani. According to this story, the chief of this ancient tribe became outraged when he discovered his daughter Mani was pregnant,
swearing vengeance on the man responsible. Mani, however, insisted she was innocent. By and by, a very light-skinned child was born and
cared for lovingly by both her mother and grandparents. Even when she died at the age of one, she was buried inside her grandparents' hut, the
spot watered every day until the white-fleshed fruit that came to be known as manioc came forth to feed the tribe. The "feeding" goes on, since
Portuguese traders from Brazil introduced cassava to their holdings on the African continent, where it is still a staple crop. Many, if not most,
traditional African dishes are made with cassava. Today, it's among the most important crops in the tropical world, from Latin America to Asia.

FILETE EN SALSA VERDE

¼ cup Peruvian pisco

¼ cup beef broth

1 tablespoon beef stock, concentrated

1 cup beef demi-glace

4 tablespoons green peppercorns in brine

2 cups heavy cream

1 cup milk

½ cup water

¼ cup all-purpose flour

¼ cup butter

1 teaspoon white pepper

4 (8-ounce) New York strip steaks

THE OLD WORLD CLASSIC FRENCH *STEAK AU POIVRE* MEETS THE NEW WORLD. PERUVIAN PISCO SEEMED THE PERFECT SPIRIT TO PLAY THE ROLE OF THE TRADITIONAL BRANDY. MOST IMPORTANT IS THE RIGHT CUT OF BEEF. WE USE ONE CALLED A CLOD TENDER. BECAUSE IT'S SO SIMILAR TO TENDERLOIN, IT'S JUST RIGHT FOR BUTTERFLYING THE WAY WE DO A CHURRASCO. THAT GIVES THE MEAT MORE SURFACE AREA FOR ABSORBING THE MARINADE, AS WELL AS FOR QUICK HIGH-HEAT, FLAVOR-SEALING COOKING.

Combine the pisco, broth and broth concentrate in a pan over high heat and stir to reduce by ⅓, about 5 minutes. Stir in the demi-glace and cook for 10 minutes. Add the peppercorns, cream, milk and water, cooking for 10 minutes more. In a separate pan, combine the flour and butter, stirring to make a light-colored roux. Add the roux to the sauce. Season with white pepper. Grill the steaks to the desired degree of doneness and serve with pisco pepper sauce spooned over the top. Serves 4.

PINEAPPLE

There is a noteworthy portrait of British King Charles II painted in 1675, in which His Majesty is shown being given the first pineapple ever grown in England. How that pineapple got there is a story that begins in the Americas. Botanists say the plant is indigenous to South America, almost certainly from the area between southern Brazil and Paraguay. The natives of those areas spread the pineapple throughout South America, and in time eventually the Caribbean, Central America and Mexico. It was cultivated by the Maya and the Aztecs, eventually being encountered by Columbus in 1493 and taken to Europe for admiration and further study. With that act, he made the pineapple plant the first bromeliad to ever leave the New World. Spaniards introduced pineapple to places like the Philippines, southern Africa, Guam and to the place it's most associated with today—Hawaii. The first commercial crop there was planted in 1886. Europe developed an early fascination with pineapple, especially as a hothouse novelty, and thus the painting of Charles II was created. Thought it obviously did not refer to the fruit, the English word "pineapple" was first recorded in 1398, describing the reproductive organs of conifer trees (now called "pine cones"). The name crossed over to the tropical fruit as early as 1664, when European explorers noted the similarity between fruit and cone. The Latin scientific name *Ananas comosus, ananas* comes from the Tupi word *nanas*, meaning "excellent fruit." In Spanish, pineapples are called *piña* or *ananá*.

BRAISED BEEF SHORT RIBS WITH JICAMA KIMCHEE

WE LOVE KOREAN KIMCHEE AND WE WANTED TO CREATE SOMETHING JUST LIKE IT TO SERVE ATOP OUR PERUVIAN ANTICUCHO-STYLE BEEF SHORTRIB: SOMETHING EXCELLENTLY SALTY, CRUNCHY, VINEGARY AND SPICY. JICAMA PROVIDED THE PERFECT START AND THE ADDITION OF THE PLANTAIN NOODLES COMPLETES THIS EXCITING JOURNEY THROUGH FLAVOR AND TEXTURE.

Prepare Jicama Kimchee 24 hours in advance, to give the pickling process time to work. Cut the jicama into 3-by-½-inch sticks. Dissolve the sugar and salt in the vinegar in a bowl, whisking. Add the pepper paste and stir to dissolve, followed by the water, garlic, green onion and jicama sticks. Transfer to an airtight container and let pickle for 24 hours.

Preheat the oven to 325° F. To make the Short Ribs, heat the oil in a large braising pot and, over high heat, brown the ribs to a deep, dark color—the secret to great flavor in any braised dish. Remove the ribs and pour off fat, leaving the bottom of the pot covered with browned bits. Add the onion, carrot, celery and tomato paste, stirring briefly while scraping up the browned bits. Return the ribs. Add the garlic and ginger, followed by the bay leaf and water, demi-glace and Coke. Cover the pot with a lid or aluminum foil. Cook in the oven for 4 hours.

Let the short ribs cool. When ready to serve, brush each rib with Anticucho Marinade and grill over high heat. Serve a mound of noodles on each of 4 dinner plates; top with 2 ribs and then with the Jicama Kimchee. Serves 4.

JICAMA KIMCHEE

½ pound peeled jicama

¼ cup sugar

2 tablespoons salt

1 ½ cup seasoned rice vinegar

½ cup Korean hot pepper paste

1 cup water

¼ cup minced garlic

½ cup chopped green onion

SHORT RIBS

2 tablespoons corn oil

8 (4-ounce) beef short ribs

½ cup chopped onion

½ chopped carrot

½ cup chopped celery

1 tablespoon tomato paste

2 tablespoons minced garlic

2 tablespoons minced ginger

1 bay leaf

1 cup water

1 cup beef demi-glace
(see recipe p. 202)

1 cup Coca-Cola

Anticucho Marinade
(see recipe p. 60)

Pan-Fried Plantain Noodles
(see recipe p. 150)

THE CHURRASCO

CHIMICHURRI

3 bunches curly parsley

6 tablespoons minced garlic

4 cups extra-virgin olive oil

1 cup white wine vinegar

2 tablespoons kosher salt

1 tablespoon black pepper

1 teaspoon dried oregano

1 (2-pound) center-cut beef tenderloin

Salt and pepper to taste

IF THERE IS ANY SIGNATURE ENTREE AT OUR RESTAURANTS, THIS IS IT. VOTED TOP 10 STEAKS IN THE U.S. BY *ESQUIRE,* IT OFTEN MAKES UP HALF OF OUR TICKET ORDERS IN THE KITCHEN. THE WORD "CHURRASCO" MEANS MANY THINGS TO PEOPLE ACROSS LATIN AMERICA, IN ARGENTINA IT'S SKIRT STEAK; IN BRAZIL, A SHOULDER CUT. WHAT WE DO WITH BEEF TENDERLOIN AND CHIMICHURRI IN OUR HOUSTON RESTAURANTS, HOWEVER, IS UNIQUE TO NICARAGUA. YOU WILL FIND IT HERE WITH US, IN A FEW NICARAGUAN PLACES IN MIAMI, AND THEN IN NICARAGUA ITSELF. THAT'S IT.

Cut the stems from the parsley and rough chop. Then combine all parsley, garlic, about 1 cup of the olive oil, the vinegar, salt, pepper and oregano in a food processor. Liquify by pulsing and let sit for at least 2 hours. Transfer the mixture to a cutting board and chop with a knife until fine and smooth. Transfer to a bowl and whisk in the remaining oil. (This recipe makes more chimichurri than you'll need for this churrasco, but nobody ever complains about having leftover chimichurri.)

Trim any visible fat and gristle from the beef tenderloin. On a cutting board, cut the tenderloin crossways into two 16-ounce halves. Set each pointing out from you and, using a sharp knife, cut downward about ¼ inch from the left side till you reach about the same distance from the bottom. Keeping the knife straight up and down, saw gently back and forth while pushing the beef to the right and creating a fairly uniform ¼-inch thick rectangle. Cut the rectangle in half to produce two approximately equal squares. Repeat with the other half of the tenderloin. Season with salt and pepper. Generously brush with chimichurri. Grill over a very hot fire to desired degree of doneness. Serve with Brown Butter Béarnaise (recipe p. 141). Serves 4.

BROWN BUTTER BÉARNAISE

In a pan, prepare the vinegar reduction by combining all ingredients over medium-high heat and reducing until nearly all liquid has evaporated. About 2 tablespoons of the shallot-vinegar mixture should be left.

Brown the butter in a pan until the color of a toasted bagel, then strain through a fine sieve to remove the dark milk solids. Over a double boiler, whisk together the egg yolks, water and wine until they resemble custard and coat the back of a spoon. (Or, swipe your finger across the bottom of the pan; the line should remain.) Whisking to emulsify, slowly add the browned butter to the egg mixture. Add the tarragon leaves and salt. Remove from heat and cover for 30 minutes. Makes about 1 quart.

VINEGAR REDUCTION

¼ cup white vinegar

1 tablespoon lemon juice

¼ cup white wine

⅓ cup diced shallot

1 tablespoon Tabasco pepper sauce

1 tarragon stem

3 sticks butter

2 egg yolks

2 tablespoons water

2 tablespoons white wine

2 tablespoons chopped tarragon leaves

½ teaspoon salt

SIDES

When it comes to the starches,

vegetables and anything else that might appear on the side of our plates, there are only two rules. The dish has got to be delicious on its own, to make you want to pick up a fork or spoon and eat it, even if there's nothing else around. And it's got to complement the main dish, which we refer to as the "center of the plate," even though sometimes it's positioned a bit off to the side. While sounding so simple and logical, these rules have consequences in the daily creation of Cordúa sides. If, for instance, a main item is big, bold and complicated, the accompaniment generally needs to be simple and lightly flavored. If, on the other hand, a main item is straightforward, as in grilled meat or seafood without much crusting, coating or saucing, the side could be big, bold and complicated. Our goal is for each item on your plate to complement the others, rather than battle for your attention. Achieving this balance is more like art than science. Just as in art, the books may say a certain color should never be used next to another, but when the painter places them together on the canvas, it's declared a masterpiece. For all our experience, we are endlessly surprised by where that balance resides.

GALLO PINTO

BEANS

1 pound dried red kidney beans

1 ½ gallons water

6 cloves garlic

1 tablespoon kosher salt

1 cup corn oil

1 cup chopped onion

RICE

1 stick unsalted butter

2 ½ cups jasmine rice

5 cups water

2 ½ teaspoons kosher salt

1 tablespoons malt vinegar

1 tablespoon habanero pepper sauce

OF ALL THE DISHES CLOSE HEART, GALLO PINTO HAS A SPECIAL PLACE. IT'S THE ONE DISH MY PARENTS WOULD SHIP TO MY SISTERS AND ME DURING COLLEGE. IT WAS ALMOST ALWAYS ON THE STOVE AT HOME AS IT IS THE STAPLE NICARAGUAN SIDE. SEEMINGLY SIMPLE. GALLO PINTO HAS A COMPLEX DEPTH FROM BLACK BEANS SLOWLY COOKED WITH ONION-FLAVORED OIL. WE SOMETIMES ADD STRIPS OF CHURRASCO MEAT FOR HEARTIER CENTER PLATE ITEM.

To cook the Beans, rinse them in water and pick out any stones. Place beans in a large pot and add the water. Bring to a boil, reduce heat, cover and simmer for 1 hour. Add the garlic and salt, cooking covered until beans are tender, 2-3 hours more. Add additional water if needed. Remove from heat and refrigerate, preferably overnight.

Prepare the Rice by melting the butter in a pot, adding rice and stirring for about 10 minutes, until toasted golden brown. Add the water and salt and cook until dry holes appear where bubbles used to be. Turn over heat and cover pot, letting rice continue to steam for an additional 10 minutes. In a bowl, combine the malt vinegar and habanero sauce. Once rice is cooked and all liquid is absorbed, pour the vinegar-pepper sauce over the top. Let cool completely.

To complete the dish, combine the corn oil with the onion in a pan large enough to hold the beans and bring to a simmer, cooking onion until caramelized, about 10 minutes. Remove the onion from the pot (reserving for another use) and add the beans to refry. Cook for 20 minutes, turning gently with a rubber spatula to avoid crushing. Mix in the cooled rice. You should have approximately twice as much rice as beans. Serves 6-8.

CILANTRO RICE

8 cups chopped cilantro
1 tablespoon minced garlic
1 ½ tablespoon corn oil
¾ cup diced yellow onion
2 cups rice
3 ½ cups chicken stock
1 ½ tablespoon salt
¾ cup diced tomatoes

THIS SIDE POPULAR AT AMAZÓN GRILL, GETS PAINTED GREEN WITH CILANTRO AND HAS A BRILLIANT KICK FROM VINEGAR AND GARLIC. THIS RECIPE WORKS BEST WITH WIDER RICE GRAINS.

Purée the cilantro with the garlic. Heat the corn oil in a large pan, then stir in the rice until it is golden. Add the chicken stock along with the cilantro-garlic mixture and the salt. Bring stock to a boil, then reduce heat and cover until rice is soft and all liquid has been absorbed, about 20 minutes. Remove from heat and stir in diced tomatoes. Serves 8.

IN TRIBUTE
Glenn Cordúa

I am in the restaurant business today because of all the misinformation, all the happy numbers, that my older brother Glenn gave me. It would take so little money, he told me, and you can make so much. And I am forever grateful for that. Glenn's guidance in the early years was essential, even though neither of us had any restaurant experience. He knew that this is what I should be doing with my life, even though it sounded like a crazy idea. All the voices in my head were telling me not to do it; Glenn's was the voice, at times the only voice, telling me that I should. And even though he was teaching psychology fulltime at the University of Houston, he gave that first Churrascos his time and talent as well. He and his wife Claire would work the door with Lucia back then. And he did everything, from introducing me to restaurant veterans to bringing in an IT contact to design our first POS system. Perhaps most of all, Glenn shared with us his love of wine, especially of Spanish and South American wines when almost nobody knew anything about them. They were perfect for our food. I look back at the stacks of press clippings we generated in those early days, and I'm always struck by how much attention we got because of Glenn and his wines. I think he saw in me, the kid brother, the man whom nobody else could see. Which was his job, *verdad*?

BLACK BEAN REFRITOS

EVERY HOUSEHOLD IN LATIN AMERICA HAS A POT OF BOILED BEANS ON THE STOVE. TO ENHANCE THEM, YOU CAN FRY THE BOILED BEANS WITH ONIONS AND OIL. AND THEN, IF YOU REALLY CARE ABOUT THE PEOPLE YOU'RE SERVING, YOU CAN FRY THE BEANS ONE MORE TIME. THE EXTRA STEP SHOWS PLENTY OF LOVE. THIS IS NOT A SPEEDY PROCESS, BUT THEN AGAIN, NEITHER IS REAL LOVE.

Pick any rocks from the beans and rinse them briefly. Combine the beans in a large pot with the water, adding the ½ cup butter and garlic. Bring to a boil, then reduce heat to a simmer and cook until beans are tender and nearly all liquid is absorbed, about 1 ½ hours. In a separate pan, sauté the bacon and onion in the manteca over medium-low heat until the bacon is crisp, about 25 minutes. Add to the black beans. Purée with a stick blender or in a food processor.

Transfer the bean purée to a large nonstick pan. Add the ¾ cup butter, Worcestershire and salt. Over medium-low heat, cook the puréed beans until as much water evaporates as possible, concentrating the flavors. When you flip the beans in the pan, it should come off the nonstick surface in a single dense, thick piece.

3 pounds dry black beans
1 ½ gallon water
½ cup butter
¼ cup minced garlic
1 pound bacon, chopped
5 cups chopped onion
¼ cup Manteca
¾ cup butter
¾ cup Worcestershire sauce
2 tablespoons salt

BEANS

In Peru, around 10,000 years ago, somebody did us all a big favor by figuring out how to domesticate the wild-growing plant that gave the world beans—almost certainly the most important source of protein to humans in history. Sometime after that, travelers seem to have introduced bean growing to Mexico—which was, in a sense, more homecoming than introduction. Food historians believe the original wild bean plant had made its own way south from the lowland tropics of Mexico to the highland Andes of Peru. Europeans became aware of beans from the Americas in the 16th century, quickly learning to distinguish them from Old World variations like lentils and favas. These hardy legumes soon became a popular European crop, being highly nutritious as well as easy to grow and store. Renaissance gourmet Bartholomew Scappi described dishes of beans, eggs, cinnamon, walnuts, sugar, onions and butter. And Catherine de' Medici was so enamored of the beans that grew in her native Italy that she smuggled some to France when she married Henry, Duke of Orléans, later to become King Henry II. We can probably thank Catherine, therefore, for the invention of cassoulet, a French dish made with beans from the Americas with goose fat, duck or lamb.

PAN-FRIED PLANTAIN NOODLES

1 ripe plantain

1 tablespoon melted butter

1 tablespoon rum

2 eggs

2 egg yolks

1 ½ cup all-purpose flour

Salt for water

1 tablespoon corn oil

½ tablespoon Achiote Marinade (see recipe p. 128)

¼ cup thinly sliced onion

¼ cup thinly sliced red better pepper

¼ cup thinly sliced poblano pepper

THESE NOODLES ARE MADE WITH RIPENED SWEET PLANTAIN AND COMPLEMENT SPICY DISHES REALLY WELL. FRESH PASTA COOKS QUICKLY SO THEY ARE BOILED AND THEN PAN FRIED FOR SOME CARAMELIZATION.

Preheat oven to 350° F. Peel the plantain. Combine the butter and rum in a bowl and brush on the plantain. Roast until golden brown and extra-sweet, about 35 minutes. Transfer to a blender with the eggs and extra yolks, blending until smooth and creamy. Gradually add the flour until a dough forms, pulls away from the sides of the bowl and becomes a ball. Wrap the dough in plastic wrap and let rest in the oven for 30 minutes.

Retrieving dough, cut the ball into 4 approximately equal pieces. Working with your hands on a clean, floured surface, press the dough quarters out enough to run through a pasta machine, starting on setting 1 and going thinner for setting 4. Fold up each time to run through again and pat on flour to correct any stickiness. Once the pasta is thin, roll it up and slice across, then unroll into long strips. Cook for about 1 minute in boiling, salted water.

Transfer from the water to a sauté pan with the corn oil and Achiote Marinade. Turn quickly to distribute color and flavor evenly. Toss the onion, bell pepper and poblano into the pan for a quick pan-fry with the noodles. Serves 4.

RUM

The spirit so many of us crave, in punches and piña coladas after encounters in the Caribbean and across Latin America, is intimately associated with two dark marks on history: colonialism and slavery. It was sugar and the pursuit thereof that gave the Americas so much appeal to the colonial powers of Europe—especially Spain, France and England—and it was sugar that made slavery what was seen then as an economic necessity. As an afterthought and certainly as a byproduct, sugar gave the world molasses, and molasses gave the world rum. No one is 100% certain how the spirit got its name, but it may be a severely shortened version of sugar's official botanical label: *Saccharum officinarm*. According to some wags, however, the three-letter word derives from *rumbustion* or *rumbullion,* archaic English words for uproar or ruckus, which makes sense. The first rum to be made from the molasses left over from refining sugar happened by accident, as natural fermentation might in all the heat of the tropics. According to legend, it was a slave who first dipped a ladle into the discarded byproduct and returned to family and friends happier than he set out. Today's quality rums come in a wide variety of colors, flavors and ages (starting out clear and taking on color via aging in oak barrels). Virtually every Caribbean islander will tell you the rum from his or her island is the best, as will rum aficionados in Nicaragua, El Salvador and Guatemala.

TAMALE GNOCCHI WITH SMOKED TOMATO SAUCE

GNOCCHI

3 ½ cups corn kernels

1 cup water

6 ½ cups instant corn masa harina

3 tablespoons kosher salt

2 tablespoons sugar

1 stick unsalted butter, melted

1 cup ricotta cheese

SMOKED TOMATO SAUCE

2 pounds fresh tomatoes, quartered

1 ½ tablespoons olive oil

Kosher salt

Freshly ground black pepper

3 teaspoons minced garlic

¼ teaspoon crushed red pepper

½ cup chicken stock

1 cup heavy cream

WE ARE ALWAYS LOOKING FOR DIFFERENT USES FOR MASA. THIS DISH CAME WITH THE OPENING OF THE WOODLANDS AMÉRICAS. IT'S GREAT AS A SIDE OR WITH A RAGOUT SMOKED TOMATO SAUCE MAKES THE CORN IN THIS DUMPLINGS TASTE TOASTED.

Combine the corn and water and purée. In a large mixing bowl, combine the masa with the salt and sugar. In a separate bowl, combine the corn purée with the butter and ricotta, then add this to the dry mixture. Thoroughly incorporate into a pasta dough. Using a pastry bag, pipe the dough out like a long sausage onto plastic wrap, then use the wrap to roll the dough even tighter. Tie the plastic wrap at the ends.

Using a perforated pan over boiling water, steam the dough in the plastic wrap for 1 hour. Let it cool, then slice into gnocchi and serve covered with Smoked Tomato Sauce (see recipe below). Serves 10.

SMOKED TOMATO SAUCE

Heat a stovetop smoker according to the manufacturer's directions. In a mixing bowl, toss the tomatoes with 1 tablespoon of olive oil, and season with salt and pepper. Place the tomatoes on the rack of the smoker over corn husks and smoke for 30 minutes. Remove the tomatoes from the smoker, reserving the tomato juices.

Heat the remaining olive oil in a medium saucepan over medium-high heat and add the garlic, cooking for 1 minute. Add the smoked tomatoes and their juices. Cook for 3-4 minutes, stirring often. Add the chicken stock and bring to a boil. Reduce the heat to a simmer and cook for about 25 minutes. Use a blender or food processor to purée the tomato mixture until smooth. Strain into a pan through a fine sieve, pressing to get all the juices. Add the cream. Simmer until slightly thickened, 5-6 minutes. Season with salt and pepper.

CORN POLENTA SPOONBREAD

HERE, THE DEEP SOUTH TRADITION OF SPOONBREAD TAKES A TOUR OF LATIN AMERICA. POLENTA IS A BEAUTIFUL FORM OF CORN, THE GRANDMOTHER OF GRITS, AND WE FOLD IN MOUNDED EGG WHITES, ALONG WITH SAUTÉED ONION, BELL PEPPER AND POBLANO, AND BAKE IT LIKE A SOUFFLÉ.

Preheat the oven to 280° F. Heat the oil in a large pot and stir together the corn, onion and green onion, bell pepper, poblano, garlic, crushed red pepper and salt. Cook until softened. Heat the milk in a large pot with the concentrated chicken stock and the bay leaf. Bring to a boil. Add the polenta, stirring until it reaches the consistency of mashed potatoes, 15-20 minutes. Remove bay leaf. Stir the sautéed vegetables into the polenta. Pour the heavy cream into a bowl and whisk in the egg yolks, then add this with the baking powder to the polenta.

In a separate bowl, beat the egg whites with the cream of tartar. Using a wide spatula, thoroughly incorporate the egg whites into the polenta as though making a soufflé. Coat a baking pan with cooking spray and pour in the polenta batter. Cover with foil and set inside a larger pan filled with hot water. Bake until set and cooked through, about 1 hour. Serves 10-12.

1 tablespoon olive oil
1 cup corn kernels
½ cup chopped yellow onion
¼ cup chopped green onion
½ cup chopped red bell pepper
½ cup chopped poblano pepper
1 teaspoon minced garlic
¼ teaspoon crushed red pepper
½ teaspoon salt
4 cups whole milk
1 tablespoon chicken stock, concentrated
1 bay leaf
1 cup polenta
1 teaspoon baking powder
1 ¼ cup heavy cream
3 eggs, separated
½ teaspoon cream of tartar

PASSION FRUIT

When 16th century Catholics explored and conquered Mexico and South America, they barely had to glance at the purple flower of the plant that gives us passion fruit before knowing just what to call it. *Flor de las cino llagas,* they declared—"flower of the five wounds." The Passion of Jesus, therefore, is a far cry from the earthbound passions that most assume the name refers to. Passion fruit is considered native to Brazil. Still, the popularity of the fruit has grown over the past four hundred years to the point that it's a crop in virtually every corner of the earth's tropical belt. It's known as *Maracuyá* in Brazil and Ecuador, *Parcha* in Venezuela, *Lilikoi* in Hawaii, and *Chinola* or *Parchita* (little Parcha) in Puerto Rico. To this day, fresh passion fruit is wildly popular in its native country. The demand is so strong that Brazilians have had to start importing from Ecuador to keep up with their own demand. The fruit is used in fresh beverages made both at home and in stalls throughout the country. Passion fruit was introduced into Hawaii in 1880 and it quickly caught on, thanks to the islands' perfect climate. In 1951, the University of Hawaii even chose it as the most promising crop for development, undertaking a program to market a frozen passion fruit juice concentrate. Though the industry was wiped out several years later by a combination of viruses, high labor costs and the skyrocketing real estate prices, it was too late. Hawaiians love passion fruit and now have to import it, registering what may be the single highest per capita consumption on earth.

QUINOA PILAF

2 cups quinoa
2 tablespoons corn oil
¼ cup diced onion
¼ cup diced carrot
¼ cup diced celery
1 tablespoon minced garlic
½ teaspoon crushed red pepper
6 cups chicken stock
1 teaspoon salt

PILAF IS TYPICALLY MADE WITH RICE, BUT AS OUR FAMILY STARTED TRYING TO EAT HEALTHIER AT OUR SUNDAY DINNERS, WE DISCOVERED THE "SUPER FOOD" CALLED QUINOA, ANOTHER GIFT OF THE AMERICAS. QUINOA IS GREAT MORE WAYS THAN WE CAN COUNT, SERVED ALONGSIDE ROAST CHICKEN, COOKED AS RISOTTO, SPRINKLED ATOP A SALAD OR EVEN PUFFED OUT LIKE RICE KRISPIES. IT'S VERSATILITY IS AMAZING.

Toast the quinoa in the oil until golden brown and giving off a wonderful nutty aroma, 5-7 minutes. Add the onion, carrot and celery and sauté until starting to soften, then stir in the garlic and crushed red pepper, cooking briefly but not burning. Add the chicken stock and the salt (Note the 3-1 liquid-quinoa ratio, rather than the 2-1 favored for cooking rice.) Boil without stirring until liquid is absorbed and dry holes form. Remove quinoa from the heat, cover with aluminum foil and let sit for 30 minutes. Serves about 8.

IN TRIBUTE
Doña Tere O'Campo

I met the amazing Doña Tere after college. Back home in Peru, she had found herself as a single mom and turned to the cooking she loved to make a living. Incredibly, she took herself all the way to Paris to study at Le Cordon Bleu, then came home to Lima to start teaching cooking classes. These classes propelled her into an illustrious career with cooking shows on Peruvian television. There's a reason Doña Tere is called the "Julia Child of Peru." By the time we opened the first Churrascos in 1988, she was living in Houston and was wanting to make desserts for us along with her daughter-in-law Ana, who happened to be my wife Lucia's sister. We, of course, weren't going to say no to my wife's sister, but we also got "the Julia Child of Peru" in the bargain. Our original *tres leches* was their handiwork, as were many other Latin desserts we served in those early years. Equally importantly, it was Doña Tere who decided I knew nothing about food until I'd tasted Peruvian food. She led me there on a trip, introduced me to chefs and restaurateurs, and gave me an approach to Latin cuisine I never could have had otherwise—decades before Peruvian became popular in the States. Peru became the country, and Doña Tere's dishes the essence, that influenced our cooking the most.

SWEET POTATO GRATIN

4 pounds sweet potatoes, peeled and thinly sliced

3 cups heavy cream

4 eggs, lightly beaten

1 teaspoon kosher salt

½ teaspoon white pepper

1 ½ cups grated cotija cheese

¼ pound roasted poblano peppers, thinly sliced

1 cup unseasoned breadcrumbs, or pulverized croutons

SWEET POTATOES ARE NATIVE TO THE AMERICAS. BUT AS A FAMILY, WE TAKE A DIFFERENT DIRECTION THAN THE TRADITIONAL THANKSGIVING DISH. I'VE NEVER UNDERSTOOD THE AMERICAN TRADITION OF ADDING MORE SUGAR TO SWEET POTATO. HERE POBLANO ADDS A GREAT SPICY COMPLEMENT.

Preheat oven to 350° F. Bring a pot of salted water to a boil and cook sliced sweet potatoes until tender, about 10 minutes. Drain the sweet potatoes, being careful not to break or tear the slices. In a mixing bowl, combine the cream, eggs, salt and white pepper. Coat a baking pan with vegetable spray and spread a layer of the cream mixture.

In order, add the sweet potato slices, about ½ the grated cheese and the poblano peppers. Finish with layers of the cream mixture, grated cheese and breadcrumbs. Coat underside of aluminum foil with vegetable spray and cover baking pan. Bake until gratin is golden brown, finishing uncovered, about 40 minutes total.

SWEET POTATO

Sweet potatoes are one of the most popular tubers native to and enjoyed in the Americas, with the true yam being far less colorful or flavorful, and not related in the least. The confusion, first recorded in this country in 1676, goes back to the African word for yam. The word varied from tribal language to tribal language, and therefore among different sets of slaves brought to the American South, often by way of the Caribbean. It might be *nyami,* or *djambi* or *njam.* Meaning nothing more specific than "to eat," the name found itself associated less and less with the original yam, and more and more with the bright orange sweet potato. One of the oldest vegetables in human history, the sweet potato was first domesticated thousands of years ago in Central America, probably somewhere between Mexico and the mouth of the Orinoco River in Venezuela. By 750 B.C., its popularity had spread to Peru, and by 1492, it had made it all the way to the Caribbean Island of St. Thomas, where historians say Columbus encountered it there. Thanks to the resulting spread to Europe and then return to colonial America, the word "potato" meant sweet potato for the longest time. The descriptive word "sweet" was added only before the Revolutionary War, to differentiate the original from the white "Irish potatoes" (also originally from Peru) that were arriving with immigrants.

AREPAS

AREPAS ARE A WONDERFUL MELDING OF BREAD AND TORTILLA THAT ARE IMMENSELY POPULAR IN VENEZUELA AND COLOMBIA. THEY CAN BE STUFFED, AND OFTEN ARE, BUT WE FEEL THEY MAINTAIN THEIR INTEGRITY BETTER WHEN SEAFOOD OR MEATS OR VEGETABLES ARE SET ON TOP. IN PARTICULAR, OUR FAMILY LOVES TO USE AREPAS AS THE BASE FOR EGGS BENEDICT, UNDER A BLANKET OF LUSH FRENCH HOLLANDAISE.

4 cups pre-cooked white cornmeal
2 teaspoons kosher salt
2 cups grated cotija cheese
2 cups grated panela cheese
4 ½ cups water
2 sticks butter

Mix cornmeal, salt and cheeses in a mixing bowl. Warm the water and butter together in a saucepan. Add liquid mixture to dry mixture, combining with gloved hands. Let cool. When ready to cook, use an ice cream scoop to take out balls of dough and press them into patties about ½ inch thick with your hands moistened with water. Working a few at a time, cook arepas on a medium-high griddle until the light golden color of biscuits, 4-5 minutes on each side. Makes about 24 arepas.

IN TRIBUTE
Jose Orlando Duque

When it comes to the service and hospitality of a Cordúa restaurant, no one understands those elements better than Duque. He came to us after working with some of the best in Houston during the economic rollercoaster of the 1980s—from La Tour d'Argent to Brennan's to a high-end nightclub or two. As a waiter, he was a crucial part of some of the best dining going on in Houston, and he brought that unique perspective to our waitstaff at the first Churrascos. It was funny: Duque was always the waiter bringing special requests back to the kitchen, to the point that other waiters (and, of course, the kitchen) started complaining. None of the other waiters were doing it. But when I talked to Duque, he told me something I'll never forget. "Michael," he said, "I'm the only one communicating the guest's perspective." Duque became the standard-bearer of what Cordúality meant in the dining room. By the time the second Churrascos opened in 1990, I chose him to be the GM. Duque is legendary.

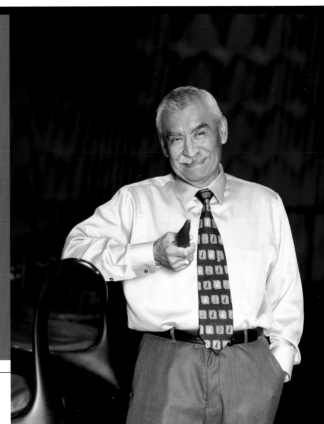

NICARAGUAN STUFFING

1 cup golden rains

4 cups whole milk

1 loaf white bread

1 (2-pound) pork shoulder, cut into 1 ½-inch cubes

½ pound bacon

1 onion, chopped

4 cloves garlic

1 pound potatoes, cooked and cubed

1 cup finely chopped Italian-style pickled giardiniera

1 cup chopped pimento-stuffed olives

3 tablespoons capers

2 eggs, lightly beaten

1 tablespoon Worcestershire sauce

2 tablespoons ketchup

2 tablespoons ground mustard

4 teaspoons ground ginger

1 teaspoon ground nutmeg

4 tablespoons white vinegar

2 tablespoons sugar

Salt and pepper to taste

1 cup unsalted butter

THIS DISH IS MADE AND SERVED IN NICARAGUA ONLY ON CHRISTMAS, THUS IT'S A CHRISTMAS-ONLY DISH FOR NICARAGUANS HERE IN THE UNITED STATES. IN AN IRONY WE TALK ABOUT OFTEN, ONE OF THE REASONS THIS IS A SPECIAL-OCCASION RECIPE IS BECAUSE IT RELIES ON SO MANY CANNED ITEMS IMPORTED INTO NICARAGUA FROM AMERICA. IT MAKES A ONE-PLATE MEAL.

In a bowl, soak the raisins in 1 cup of the milk. Tear white bread into bite-sized chunks; mix with the raisins and remaining milk. Soak overnight in the refrigerator. Also the night before serving, cook the pork shoulder, bacon, onion and garlic in a large pot of simmering water until meat is cooked through, 20-30 minutes. Set in the broth in the refrigerator overnight.

The next day, strain and reserve the cooking liquid from the meat. Roughly chop the boiled vegetables and combine in a large bowl with all remaining ingredients except butter. Melt the butter in a large skillet (or two smaller ones at the same time) and the dressing mixture. Over medium-high heat, cook the dressing until it gives up its liquid and goes from pale to golden to brown, stirring often to lift the caramelized sections to the top. This takes a long time, 2-3 hours. Serves 14-16.

CHAYOTE (MIRLITON SQUASH)

There aren't many foods of the Americas that are called as many different things in as many different places as the chayote, a member of the gourd family along with melons, cucumbers and squash. Across the Caribbean and its related slave culture around New Orleans, it's known as *christophene* (Jamaica), *mirleton* (Creole/Cajun), *chuchu* (Brazil) and *güisquil* (El Salvador), as well as pear squash or vegetable pear in the United States. *Chayote* is originally native to Mexico and Central America, where it grows abundantly and traditionally has little commercial value. It has, however, been introduced as a crop all over Latin America, and worldwide. The main growing regions today are Brazil and Costa Rica, with only the Mexican state of Veracruz getting into the business in a significant way and becoming the main exporter to the U.S. market. The chayote figures in many Latin American cuisines. The word *chayote* is a Spanish derivative of the Nahuatl word *chayohtli*. Most people regard it as having a very mild flavor by itself, so it is commonly served with seasonings like salt, pepper and butter, or else it's boiled, stewed, stuffed, mashed, baked, fried or pickled in a vinegar-based *escabeche* sauce. Occasionally in the Americas, chayote is chopped up raw and added to salads, more for texture than taste.

SWEETS

From the top of Mexico to the tip of South America, desserts tend to be very sweet and very rich. Sometimes in restaurants here or in Europe, you hear diners complain about a dessert being "too sweet." Those are words you're not likely to hear in Latin America—or by extension, in any of our restaurants. Perhaps it's because many parts of the New World grew, and still grow, sugar, making it and its sidelines like syrup and molasses an easy product to find affordably all year long. And poor refrigeration helped sweet canned products like condensed and evaporated milk become a large part of our Latin flavor profile. The sweet rich tradition set the stage for our own original tres leches, a dish that's been copied more often than any other we have created. When it comes to desserts, no other fact makes our family as happy as that one.

THE ORIGINAL TRES LECHES

SPONGE CAKE

7 eggs

2 cups sugar

2 cups flour

2 tablespoons baking powder

½ cup milk

MILKS

3 cups condensed milk

3 cups evaporated milk

3 cups heavy cream

2 tablespoon vanilla

MERINGUE

1 cup egg whites

1 teaspoon cream of tartar

2 cups sugar

1 cup water

1 teaspoon vanilla

EVERY LATIN AMERICAN COUNTRY MAKES SOME CLAIM TO INVENTING TRES LECHES. BUT AS BEST WE CAN TELL, THE RECIPE WAS INVENTED BY NESTLÉ® TO SELL MORE CANS OF CONDENSED MILK. WE MADE A LOT OF IMPROVEMENTS TO THE TRADITIONAL RECIPE, AND OUR TRES LECHES BECAME THE FIRST TO FIND AN AUDIENCE IN TEXAS. DEVELOPED WITH HELP FROM MY AUNT, ANA RUZO, THIS DELICIOUS VERSION HAS APPEARED PROUDLY ON OUR MENU AT CHURRASCOS SINCE DAY ONE, TWENTY-FIVE YEARS AGO. OUR RECIPE MAKES FOR MORE REFINED CAKE, THE BATTER FULL OF WHIPPED EGGS THAT CAUSE IT TO RISE LIKE A SOUFFLÉ IN THE OVEN.

To prepare the cake, preheat oven to 350° F. Whip the eggs in an electric mixer until fluffy, 5-7 minutes. Add the sugar under creamed, about 3 minutes. Sift together the dry ingredients and gradually add to the mixer. Reduce the speed and add the milk a little at a time. Mix at low speed for 10 minutes. Remove from mixer and pour into greased 9 X 13 X 2 ½ inch cake mold. Bake in the oven for 30 minutes, then lower heat to 325° F and bake an additional 20 minutes, until top of cake is nicely browned.

Meanwhile, combine the milks, cream and vanilla, whisking until smooth, 3-4 minutes. Remove cake from oven and, using a serrated cake knife, slice off brown top (this makes a nice, crisp snack for the baker). Pour the milk mixture over the top. Let the cake soak for about 20 minutes. Prepare the meringue by heating the sugar and water to 240° F in a saucepan, then removing from heat. Beat the egg whites with the cream of tartar in a mixer on high until soft peaks form, about 3 minutes, then slowly add the syrup.

Add vanilla and keep mixing on slow speed until the bowl cools to the touch, about 15 minutes. Pour excess milk from cake and top with meringue. Use the tines of a fork to draw wavy ridges lengthwise across the cake for decoration. Cut into squares. Serves 15.

DELIRIO DE CHOCOLATE

CHOCOLATE MOUSSE

2 pounds semisweet chocolate

2 sticks butter

1 ½ cup heavy cream

¼ cup sugar

1 cup water

8 sheets gelatin

10 egg yolks

3 cups heavy cream

TRUFFLE CAKE

2 cups cake flour

3 cups sugar

½ cup dark cocoa powder

1 ¾ tablespoons baking soda

8 eggs

1 ⅛ cups olive oil

¾ cup sour cream

1 pint heavy cream

GANACHE

1 ½ cups heavy cream

¼ cup sugar

¼ cup corn syrup

⅛ stick butter

¾ pound semisweet chocolate

WE HAD A CHOCOLATE *TRES LECHES* ON THE MENU WHEN WE OPENED ARTISTA, BUT OUR GUESTS WANTED SOMETHING EVEN MORE INTENSELY CHOCOLATE. NO ONE TASTING OUR DELIRIO CAN SAY WE'RE SHY ABOUT CHOCOLATE. SOME, IN FACT, ASK FOR A GLASS OF MILK.

To prepare the mousse, melt the chocolate with the butter in the top of a double boiler, then let cool to room temperature. Dissolve the sugar in the water in a heavy saucepan and heat until this syrup registers 220° F on a thermometer. Soften the gelatin sheets in a bowl of ice-cold water. In a separate bowl, whisk together the eggs yolks until ribbons form. Whisk the softened gelatin into the syrup, then add a little of this to the yolks to temper, then add the rest. Gradually combine this with the chocolate. In a chilled metal bowl, whip the heavy cream until thickened. Add some whipped cream to the mousse to temper, then add the rest by folding gently. Refrigerate for at least 3 hours.

To make the truffle cake, preheat oven to 300° F. Sift together the flour, sugar, cocoa powder and baking soda. In a large bowl, using a hand mixer, beat eggs for 2 minutes, then gradually add the olive oil, mixing for 6-7 minutes. Combine the sour cream with the heavy cream and beat into the liquid mixture, about 3 minutes more. Beat in sifted dry ingredients ¼ at a time until fully incorporated, about 3 minutes. Spray 2, 18 X 13 X 2 inch, baking sheets with cooking spray and line with parchment paper. Spread cake batter evenly with spatula. Bake for 25 minutes. Remove and cool on a rack.

To make the Ganache, bring the cream to a boil with the sugar, corn syrup and butter. Remove from the heat and, in a large mixing bowl, pour over the chocolate to melt. Stir until smooth and incorporated. Let cool.

Using an 11 X 16 X 2 inch cake mold, cut a rectangle from the center of the cake in the baking pan. Discard edges. Spread the cake with an approximate 1-inch layer of the chilled mouse, which will be thick, then pour warm ganache over the top and allow to set, about 5 minutes. Slice into 2 X 5 inch pieces. Makes 36 pieces.

COCOA TARTS

SOME OF MY FAVORITE DESSERTS REMIND ME OF CANDY BARS. THERE'S DEFINITELY A BIT OF NOSTALGIA IN THESE INDIVIDUAL TARTS. THE KEY TO THE FLAVOR IS THE GIANDUJA, AN ITALIAN HAZELNUT CHOCOLATE THAT WILL REMIND SOME OF NUTELLA. WE SERVE IT WITH COCONUT ICE CREAM, WHICH BRINGS IT INTO MOUNDS BAR TERRITORY.

Preheat oven to 325° F. To prepare the tart shells, cut the butter into 1-inch cubes and cream with the sugar and egg yolks in a mixer, 8-10 minutes. In a bowl, sift together the flour and cocoa powder, then add to the mixing bowl and mix until the dough forms a ball. Wrap the ball in plastic and chill in refrigerator for 1 hour.

Once chilled, let return to room temperature and scoop ¼–cup portions. Press each flat in a tortilla press lined with plastic, or roll out thin with a rolling pin. Spray 4-inch inch tart shell molds with vegetable spray and press a circle of dough into each mold. Trim off edges. Set the filled tart molds into the oven and "blind bake" (with no filling) until lightly golden, about 5 minutes. Let cool.

To make the two separate ganache fillings, use the same technique. Heat the cream in a saucepan to a low boil, add the chocolate pieces and stir until melted. Transfer to a microwave-safe bowl or cup with a spout for pouring. To complete the tarts, pour the dark chocolate ganache about halfway up the inside of each tart shell. Let cool until that layer is firm. Then, microwaving if necessary to have a pourable consistency, pour the semisweet chocolate layer atop the dark chocolate. Chill for at least 1 hour before serving. Makes 12 individual tarts.

TART SHELL
½ pound butter
¾ cup sugar
⅓ cup egg yolks
2 ½ cups all-purpose flour
½ cup cocoa powder

DARK GANACHE
12 ounces dark chocolate, broken into pieces
1 ½ cups heavy cream

SEMISWEET GANACHE
12 ounces semisweet chocolate, broken into pieces
1 ½ cups heavy cream

TEQUILA BREAD PUDDING

TOASTED BREAD

8 Sheila Partin sweet sourdough bun, or Hawaiian bread

1 cup melted butter

3 ½ teaspoon ground cinnamon

PUDDING MIX

6 eggs

4 egg yolks

½ cup sugar

¼ cup condensed milk

1 cup milk

1 cup heavy cream

1 cup half and half

1 cinnamon stick

3 tablespoons tequila

LIME CARAMEL SAUCE

½ cup sugar

¼ cup water

1 teaspoon lime juice

2 tablespoons butter

½ cup heavy cream

TEQUILA CRÈME ANGLAISE

½ cup tequila

2 cups heavy cream

3 eggs

1 cup sugar

¼ cup butter, cubed

THERE IS A NICARAGUAN VERSION OF BREAD PUDDING, NAMED FOR POPE PIUS X, BUT AT AMERICAS WE OPT FOR A MORE TRADITIONAL SOUTHERN VERSION USING SWEET SOURDOUGH MADE BY HOUSTON BAKER SHEILA PARTIN. AND WE LOVE WHAT HAPPENS TO CARAMEL, LONG THE PROVINCE OF BRANDY OR BOURBON, WHEN WE ADD A BIT OF AÑEJO TEQUILA.

Preheat the oven to 350º F. Cut the buns or bread into 1-inch cubes and toss with the melted butter. Spread cubes out on a baking pan and set in the oven until lightly toasted, about 20 minutes. Sprinkle with the ground cinnamon.

Meanwhile, lower the oven to 300º F. Prepare the pudding mix by warming the half and half in a pan with the cinnamon stick. Whisk the eggs and extra yolks in a large metal mixing bowl, then incorporate the condensed milk, followed by the milk and then the cream, whisking to incorporate each. Remove the cinnamon stick from the warmed half and half and add the liquid to the mixture. Add the tequila. Using your hands, thoroughly combine the toasted bread cubes with the pudding mix. Let soak for 10-15 minutes, until liquid is absorbed. Divide evenly into 12 ramekins and arrange in a baking pan. Cover with aluminum foil and set this inside a larger pan with water filled halfway up the sides to create a bain marie. Bake for 55 minutes.

While bread pudding is baking, prepare the two sauces. For the Lime Caramel, combine the sugar in a pan with the water and lime juice and cook until golden brown, 5-7 minutes. Whisk in the butter, being careful not to splatter. Then whisk in the cream until the sauce is smooth.

To make the Tequila Crème Anglaise, warm the tequila in a pan and then ignite it carefully, letting all the alcohol burn off. Over a double boiler, combine the remaining tequila with the cream. Beat the eggs in a mixing bowl, then beat in the sugar. Once the tequila cream has thickened, whisk in the egg-sugar mixture and let warm. Add the butter a little bit at a time, whisking over the double boiler until smooth and thickened.

Serve the individual bread puddings warm drizzled with the crème anglaise and the lime caramel sauce. Serves 12.

PASTEL DE PIÑA

FILLING

4 cups diced pineapple in juice

1 cup sugar

1 stick cinnamon

2 whole cloves

¼ cup unsalted butter

1 tablespoon vanilla

CRUST

⅔ cup unsalted butter

2 cups all-purpose flour

1 teaspoon salt

2 tablespoons shortening

¼ cup cold water

PASTEL DE PIÑA IS TO NICARAGUA WHAT APPLE PIE IS TO THE UNITED STATES. IT'S A VERY TRADITIONAL PIE, WITH A SWEET FRUIT FILLING BENEATH A DELICATE LATTICE-WORK CRUST. THE KEY TO THE FILLING IS COOKING THE PINEAPPLE OVER LOW HEAT FOR A LONG TIME, SINCE IT NEEDS TO BREAK DOWN AND TURN GOLDEN BROWN. ONLY THEN, WHEN ALMOST A MARMALADE, IS IT READY TO POUR INTO YOUR *PASTEL.*

Prepare the pie filling by combining the diced pineapple and its juice with the sugar, cinnamon and clove in a non-stick skillet and cook over low heat until a deep caramelized golden color, about 45 minutes. Pick out cinnamon and clove. Mash pineapple pieces with potato masher or fork. Stir in butter and vanilla until the butter melts. Cool about 15 minutes more. Let cool to room temperature.

To make the pie crust, cut the butter into cubes and chill in the refrigerator. Combine the flour and salt in a food processor and pulse briefly, then add the butter and shortening. Pulse 8-10 times until incorporated. Add cold water a little at a time, until a ball is formed by pulsing. Finish forming ball with your hands and wrap in plastic wrap. Chill in the refrigerator for 30 minutes.

Preheat the oven to 350° F. Take out and unwrap the dough; cut it half. Roll out one half to a ¼-inch-thick circle and use to line the bottom of a pie tin. Pour the pineapple filling into the tin. Roll out the remaining dough to the same thickness, cutting into long strips to arrange as lattice-work over the top of the pie. Bake until golden brown, 30-40. Serves 6-8. Works well, too as 6 individual tarts.

SWEET CORN FLAN

NATIVE AMERICANS HAD A LONG TRADITION OF MAKING CORN PUDDING, AND THE SPANIARDS CONTINUE THEIR TRADITION OF MAKING THE CREAMY CUSTARD THEY CALL FLAN. WE PULLED THE TWO WONDERFUL RECIPES INTO A SINGLE FOCUS. OUR FAMILY LOVES FEW THINGS MORE THAN SALTY POPCORN AND SWEET CANDY CORN. THIS FLAN BORROWS A BIT FROM BOTH.

Preheat oven to 300° F. Prepare the Caramel by cooking the sugar with the water and vanilla over medium-high heat until it turns a deep golden brown, tilting the pan and swirling the molten liquid occasionally. When finished, spoon the caramel onto the bottoms of ramekins or other ovenproof dishes. We use long rectangular dishes that hold about ¾ cup for our flan presentation.

Prepare the Corn Pudding by blending the corn with the water until smooth, then straining the purée into a bowl for a blender. Pour the milk through the sieve to help this process. In the blender, combine the corn-milk mixture with the condensed milk, cream cheese, eggs and extra yolk, blending on low speed until smooth. Divide the flan batter over the ramekins or serving dishes with caramel. Set these in a larger pan and set in the oven. Fill halfway up the sides of the dishes with water, creating a *bain-marie.* Bake for 1 hour. Allow to cool before serving. Makes 4-6 flans, depending on size of dish.

CARAMEL

⅓ cup sugar

2 tablespoons water

½ teaspoon vanilla extract

CORN PUDDING

1 ⅓ cup fresh or frozen corn kernels

2 tablespoon water

1 cup whole milk

¾ cup condensed milk

⅓ cup cream cheese

2 large eggs

1 egg yolk

VANILLA

Popularly, vanilla is known as the "world's only edible orchid," and that it is, in a manner of speaking. Though most of the world's vanilla now comes from Madagascar and a couple other islands in the Indian Ocean, it was born as a flavor in the Americas. Huge portions of the world's vanilla supply are directed into the fragrance industry. The name vanilla comes from the Spanish word *vainilla,* meaning "little pod." The mature bean filled with intensely flavored seeds is also sometimes called "the black flower," since it shrivels and turns black shortly after it is picked. The first keepers of vanilla may have been the Totonaco of the Mexican Gulf Coast, near today's Vera Cruz. In the 15th century, these Indians were conquered by the Aztecs, who brought it back to the central highlands and started using it in foods and beverages both hot and cold. Cortez conquered the vanilla crop right along with the Aztecs, bringing pods back to the court of Spain, where it was consumed exclusively by the upper crust for eighty years. It was the apothecary to Queen Elizabeth I of England who, in 1602, recommended vanilla's use all by itself, rather than as an adjunct to chocolate, and the world's two favorite tastes were liberated from each other. For centuries, cultivation of vanilla depended on pollination by a Mexican species of bee. In 1841, a 12-year-old slave on the French island of Réunion discovered how to pollinate by hand, opening history's door to large vanilla plantation not only in the Indian Ocean but on the island of Tahiti and indeed back home in Mexico.

PECAN PIE STEAMED BUN

1 whole pecan pie
1 cup milk
½ cup sugar
1 package Chinese flour
(from Asian market)
1 tablespoon corn oil
2 cups prepared dulce de leche

AS WITH SO MANY OF OUR SAVORY DISHES, THE INTERNATIONAL QUALITY OF HOUSTON LIFE INSPIRES THIS UNEXPECTED DESSERT. REMEMBER THE EXPERIENCE OF THE CHINESE "PORK BUN," ITS SAVORY FILLING SURROUNDED BY PILLOW-LIKE BREAD MADE WITH SUPER-FINE CHINESE FLOUR. THEN IMAGINE BITING INTO SUCH BUN AND DISCOVERING PECAN PIE.

Purchase your favorite pecan pie. Pulverize the pie in a food processor until it becomes a paste with bits of crunch from the nuts and crust. Prepare the steam bun dough by combining the milk, sugar and Chinese flour in a mixer with a dough hook. Knead for 20 minutes, until it forms a smooth ball. Add the oil and knead 10 minutes more. Proof the dough by covering with a clean towel and setting it in a warm spot for 30 minutes.

Roll the dough out into a "snake" and slice crossways into ¼-inch thick discs. Spread the discs out and spoon about 1 tablespoon of the pecan piece into the center, pull up the sides and seal with a twist. Set in a bamboo steamer over boiling water and steam for 10 minutes. Serve with *dulce de leche* caramel. Makes about 36 buns.

PECANS

The only major tree nut that grows in the wild in North America, the pecan is found in history as far back as the 1500s. The name "pecan" is a Native American word of Algonquin origin that was used to describe "all nuts requiring a stone to crack." With roots in central and eastern North America, as well as along the river valleys of Mexico, pecans were widely used as food before the arrival of European explorers. They were accessible to and from waterways (indeed they tended to grow along them, taking advantage of the moisture in dry areas) and much easier to shell than other American nut species. Many Native American tribes relied on wild pecans as a food source during autumn. One of the first known cultivated pecan plantings, by Spanish colonists and Franciscan friars in northern Mexico, appears to have taken place in the late 1600s. The first U.S. pecan planting took place in Long Island, New York, in 1772. By the late 18th century, pecans were growing across the Eastern Seaboard, including in the Virginia gardens of Thomas Jefferson and George Washington. During that same period, the French and Spanish colonists settling along the Gulf of Mexico, including New Orleans and Mobile, realized the value of pecans, and by 1802 the French were exporting pecans to their islands in the West Indies. From its strategic position near the mouth of the Mississippi River, New Orleans became a major center for growing, enjoying and exporting pecans. The city also spurred the development of official pecan orchard, which helped transform the long-wild or semi-wild gift of nature into a dependable cash crop.

BLUEBERRY-COCONUT SCONES

5 tablespoons butter

2 tablespoons sugar

1 cup heavy cream

2 cups all-purpose flour

1 tablespoon baking powder

½ teaspoon salt

1 cup blueberries

1 ½ cup toasted coconut

THESE SCONES WERE DEVELOPED FOR LADIES LUNCHEONS THAT WE FREQUENTLY CATER AT TOOTSIE'S, A HIGH-END LADIES CLOTHING STORE HERE IN HOUSTON. BOTH THE COCONUT AND BLUEBERRIES HELP KEEP THEM CAKEY AND MOIST.

Preheat the oven to 400° F. In the bowl of a food processor with a paddle or leaf attachment, cream the butter with the sugar, then add the cream and continue processing until smooth. Add the flour, baking, powder and salt, continuing to beat until thoroughly incorporated. Add the blueberries and coconut at the end, stirring only to combine.

Using your hands, remove the dough from the food processor and form it into a log. Slice the log crosswise into circles, and then slice each circle in half to form a half-moon shape. Arrange the half moons on a cookie sheet coated with cooking spray. Bake until the scones are golden, 15-20 minutes. Makes about 12 scones.

CHOCOLATE-BRAZIL NUT BISCOTTI

BISCOTTI ARE THE KINGS OF ITALIAN COOKIES. THE NAME GIVES AWAY THE COOKING METHOD, MEANING "TWICE COOKED." THE RESULT IS SOMETHING BOTH CRUNCHY AND CHEWY. WE PREFER THE MORE OIL-RICH NUTS—MACADAMIA, WALNUTS OR BRAZIL NUTS—WHEN WE MAKE BISCOTTI, BECAUSE THEY KEEP THE COOKIES MOIST. HERE WE MIX BRAZIL NUTS WITH CHOCOLATE.

6 tablespoons butter

1 cup sugar

2 eggs

2 cups flour

½ cup cocoa powder

1 teaspoon baking soda

1 teaspoon salt

¾ cup chocolate chips

1 cup roughly chopped Brazil nuts

Preheat the oven to 350° F. Using a food processor with a paddle attachment, cream the butter with the sugar until smooth. Then add the eggs and continue to whip. Add the flour, cocoa powder, baking soda, salt and chocolate chips, processing to form a smooth dough. Add the Brazil nuts last, so they remain in chunks.

Using your hands, form the dough into a log about ½ inch thick with a flat top and bottom, and set at the center of a baking sheet coated with vegetable spray. Bake for 25 minutes, then remove from oven and cool slightly. Slice the mostly baked dough into ½ inch strips, set these on pan and return to the oven for 10 minutes more. Remove and let crispen as they cool. Makes about 36 biscotti.

CHOCOLATE

For many, the gift of chocolate made the search for the New World worth all the difficulties. Chocolate is everywhere today. But it wasn't always so. Two millennia ago, it was only in Mesoamerica, in the form of seeds encased within pods of the cacao tree. The first people known to have made chocolate were the ancient cultures of Mexico and Central America. These people, including both Aztec and Maya at various times, mixed the ground seeds with various seasonings to make a spicy, bitter, frothy drink. In one of the most enduring Aztec legends, people lucky enough to possess the beverage spread it across floes of ice and snow in the cold, high mountains, thus hardening the liquid into something they could bite into. After their takeover, conquistadors carried the seeds back home to Spain, where new (sweeter) recipes were created. Eventually, the drink's popularity spread throughout Europe. Spanish occupiers claimed the Aztec's supply of cacao and began to demand it from the same indigenous peoples from whom the Aztecs had, during their heyday, gathered tribute. Keeping up with the European chocolate market required the labor of millions of people tending, harvesting and processing both cacao and the sugar that increasingly kept it company. For close to three hundred years, enslaved people provided most of this labor. And the first, if hardly the last, people enslaved for the sake of chocolate were Mesoamericans, the very people who invented it.

TRES LECHES PANCAKES

MILKS

3 cups condensed milk

3 cups evaporated milk

3 cups heavy cream

2 tablespoon vanilla

MERINGUE

1 cup egg whites

1 teaspoon cream of tartar

2 cups sugar

1 cup water

1 teaspoon vanilla

PANCAKES

2 cups all-purpose flour

3 tablespoons sugar

4 teaspoons baking powder

1 teaspoon kosher salt

2 cups milk

4 tablespoons butter, melted

2 eggs, lightly beaten

Vegetable spray

Extra butter

Dulce de leche

Powdered sugar

THIS IS EXACTLY WHAT IT SOUNDS LIKE AND DOESN'T DISAPPOINT. FIRST CREATED AS A BRUNCH ITEM THEY ARE A FAMILY FAVORITE WORTH GETTING OUT OF BED FOR.

To make the meringue combine the milks, cream and vanilla, whisking until smooth, 3-4 minutes. Prepare the meringue by heating the sugar and water to 240° F in a saucepan, then removing from. Beat the egg whites with the cream of tartar in a mixer on high until soft peaks form, about 3 minutes, then slowly add the syrup. Add vanilla and keep mixing on slow speed until the bowl cools to the touch, about 15 minutes.

For the pancakes, in a small bowl, whisk together the flour, sugar, baking powder and salt. In a medium bowl, whisk together the milk, butter and egg. Add the dry ingredients to the liquid to form a batter. Do not overmix. A few small lumps are fine. Heat a large nonstick skillet coated with vegetable spray and 2-3 tablespoons of butter. Cook the pancakes, each with about 3 tablespoons of batter. Fit 2-3 at a time into a large skillet, but be careful they remain separate. Cook until the pancake starts to set and bubbles open on the surface, 1-2 minutes, then flip carefully and cook 1-2 minutes more. Transfer pancakes to 200° F oven to keep warm.

When ready to serve, prepare the tres leches milk mixture and the Italian meringue as for the dessert tres leches. Quickly make 8 stacks of 3 pancakes each and use a knife to cut a large X in the top of each stack. Pour in the milk mixture until pancakes are soaked, then use a pastry bag to pipe in meringue. Drizzle with *dulce de leche* and dust with powdered sugar. Serves 8.

ALFAJORES

1 ½ cup all-purpose flour
4 tablespoons powdered sugar
1 ½ sticks butter, stiff from freezer
1 (13.4-ounce) can *dulce de leche*
Additional flour
Powdered sugar

ALFAJORES ARE THE SIMPLEST OF SHORTBREAD COOKIES, MADE OF JUST FLOUR, BUTTER AND SUGAR. THEY DISSOLVE THE SECOND YOU PUT THEM IN YOUR MOUTH, LEAVING YOU WITH LUSH, CARAMELIZED *DULCE DE LECHE.* WE PICTURE THIS WONDERFUL MILK CANDY BEING MADE IN LATIN AMERICA BY GRANDMOTHERS PATIENTLY STIRRING MILK WITH SUGAR OVER AN OPEN FIRE. LESS ROMANTICALLY, YOU CAN BOIL A CAN OF CONDENSED MILK IN BOILING WATER AND GET THE SAME TERRIFIC RESULT. OR, YOU CAN SIMPLY BUY *DULCE DE LECHE* AT THE SUPERMARKET.

Preheat oven to 300° F. Combine the flour and sugar in the bowl of a mixer, pulsing a few times until incorporated. Cut the butter in small cubes and add to the bowl, running the mixer on low speed until a ball of dough forms, about 5 minutes. Remove the ball and smooth it with your hands, then break it into several pieces. On a clean, floured surface, roll out the dough very thin—about as thin as you can. Using a 1 ½-inch pastry ring, cook out cookies that resemble half dollars. Set them not touching on a baking pan lined with parchment. Bake for 20 minutes. Let cool. Make little sandwiches by using a pastry bag or spoon to place on a small amount of *dulce de leche* on one cookie then topping them with another. Lightly dust cookie sandwiches with powdered sugar. Makes about 48.

AMARANTH

As we see with quinoa and other pleasantly chewy, nutty-tasting grains, amaranth reflects the Americas' ancient embrace of taking nutrition from the field. The Aztecs, Incas and Mayas considered amaranth their staple food, with maize (corn) and beans. In the heydey of those civilizations, amaranth was one of the most important crops in the Americas. Known to the Aztecs as *huautli,* it is thought to have represented up to 80% of their caloric consumption before the Spanish conquest. Consumed by the Inca, still today in the Andes amaranth is known as *Kiwicha.* Another important use of amaranth throughout the Americas has traditionally been for ritual drinks and foods. During the Aztec month of *Panquetzaliztli* (December 7-26), people decorated their homes and trees with paper flags and held ritual races, processions, dances, songs, prayers and finally, human sacrifices. A statue of the god was made out of amaranth seeds and honey; and at the end of the month, it was cut into small pieces so everybody could partake. After the Spanish conquest, cultivation of amaranth was outlawed, to suppress native beliefs, though some festivities were gathered into Christmas. Amaranth cultivation was preserved in hard-to-reach areas of mountainous Central and South America. Today, amaranth grains are toasted much like popcorn and mixed with honey, molasses or chocolate to make a treat called *alegría,* meaning joy in Spanish.

DRINKS

We approach the creation of cocktails not so much as bartenders but as chefs. The same rules and requirements for balance that we apply to each menu item applies to every cocktail we offer. We've been cheered by the new respect given to mixology recently, whether it's to classics from before Prohibition to the kookiest new combination being shaken or stirred down the street. Since our cocktails take inspiration from the drinking traditions of Latin America, they are refreshing rather than heavy or warm. We are always searching out delicious ingredients, from the newer, small-batch versions of rum, tequila, cachaca, pisco or bourbon, or components that we've committed to making in-house, such as our piloncillo simple syrup or our tonic water. We love cocktails. A toast to you as you add flavor to your festivities!

MOJITO

6 pieces lime cut in ⅛s

8 mint leaves

1 ½ ounces simple syrup or agave nectar

2 ounces white rum

Crushed ice

Splash of soda

1 lime wedge

1 mint leaf

Muddle lime and mint with simple syrup. Add the rum and shake with crushed ice for 10 seconds. Pour into a Collins or Highball glass. Top with soda. Stir with straw then add a second straw. Garnish with lime wedge and mint leaf.

CUCUMBER GIN MOJITO

Muddle lime and cucumber with mint and dill in simple syrup. Add rum and shake with ice for 10 seconds. Pour into a Collins glass and top with soda.

SPARKLING STRAWBERRY MOJITO

Muddle the strawberry and lime with the mint in the simple syrup. Add the rum and shake with ice for 10 seconds. Pour into a Collins glass. Top with sparkling wine.

CUCUMBER GIN MOJITO

6 pieces lime cut in ⅛s

¼ cucumber, thinly sliced

4 mint leaves

1 sprig dill

1 ½ ounces simple syrup or agave nectar

2 ounces gin

Splash of soda

SPARKLING STRAWBERRY MOJITO

2 strawberries

4 pieces lime cut in ⅛s

5 mint leaves

1 ½ ounces simple syrup or agave nectar

2 ounces aged rum

Crushed ice

1 ounce Segura Viudas Brut Reserva Cava

BOURBON

In all of our enthusiasm for foods, spirits and other things that were discovered or created in Latin American, we shouldn't forget one other spirit from a world that never knew Aztec, Maya or Inca, that was never overrun by Spanish conquistadors. Bourbon is whiskey from the state of Kentucky—unless of course it's "sippin' whiskey" from across the line in Tennessee. From the spirit's beginnings in the late 1700s, bourbon has been made with that great American staple, corn. The making of this whiskey was no accident. Life on the frontier near the Ohio and Mississippi Rivers was challenging, and the frontiersmen found they needed a diversion. As many came to the region from places like Scotland and Ireland, they knew how to turn whatever was at hand into alcohol, and what was available was corn. Earlier pioneers of bourbon include Evan Williams and Jacob "Jim" Beam, whose names retain some immortality on bottles behind bar tops. The aging of freshly distilled bourbon in oak barrels probably *did* happen by accident, perhaps a happy accident of waiting in wood on a dock for shipment south down the Mississippi to New Orleans. Bardstown, Kentucky's second-oldest city, may have been its *first*-oldest when it comes to distillation. Other proto-producers settled in what was known as Old Bourbon County, thus giving a legendary American spirit its unique flavor and, of course, its legendary name.

Sparkling Strawberry Mojito

COCONUT HIBISCUS BATIDA

1 ½ ounces aged rum

½ ounce cachaca

1 ounce orange juice

1 ounce pineapple juice

1 ounce Coco Real cream
of coconut

½ ounce Monin Hibiscus Syrup

Ice cubes

Shaved coconut for garnish

Combine all ingredients and shake with ice cubes. Strain into a rocks glass and garnish with shaved coconut.

CAIPIRINHA

6 pieces lime cut in ⅛s

2 ounces simple syrup or agave nectar

1 ½ ounces cachaca

Crushed ice

Splash of soda

Lime wedge for garnish

Muddle the lime in the simple syrup. Add the cachaca and shake with crushed ice for 10 seconds. Pour into a rocks glass. Add sodas and stir. Garnish with lime wedge.

DARK BERRY CAIPIRINHA

4-6 blueberries

2 blackberries

2 lemon wedges, sliced into quarters

½ ounce honey

½ ounce amaretto

1 ½ ounce Kentucky bourbon

Muddle the berries first, then add the lemons, honey, mint and amaretto and muddle again. Add the bourbon, stir and pour over ice.

Coconut Hibiscus Batida

Paloma

PALOMA

Muddle the grapefruit and lime with the simple syrup. Add tequila and shake with ice for 5 seconds. Strain into a rocks glass with a salted rim. Top with grapefruit soda and stir. Garnish with grapefruit wheel.

Add a twist by freezing grapefruit juice in an ice cube tray for a progressive cocktail.

4 pieces grapefruit cut into $1/16$s
4 pieces lime cut into $1/8$s
$1/2$ ounce simple syrup (see recipe p. 203)
1 $1/2$ ounces blanco tequila
Ice cubes
Salt, if desired
3 ounces grapefruit soda
1 half-moon slice grapefruit

MARGARITA

1 lime, cut in $1/8$s
2 pieces orange cut in $1/8$s
1 ounce simple syrup (see recipe p. 203)
1 $1/2$ ounces blanco tequila
1 ounce triple sec
Ice
Salt
1 lime wedge for garnish

Muddle the lime and orange with the simple syrup. Add tequila and triple sec. Shake for 5 seconds and pour over ice in a salt-rimmed rocks glass. Garnish with lime wedge.

GINGER TEQUILA PUNCH

2 pieces orange cut in $1/8$s
$1/2$ ounce simple syrup (seed recipes p. 203)
1 ounce blanco tequila
1 ounce Cuarenta Tres Licor
$1/2$ ounce lemon juice
Ice cubes
1 ounce ginger ale
1 pinch ground cinnamon

Muddle the orange in the simple syrup. Add liquors and lemon juice. Shake with ice and strain into a rocks glass. Top with ginger ale and stir. Sprinkle with cinnamon.

TEQUILA

In recent years, nearly all of us have had a thing or two to learn about tequila, the spirit most associated with Mexico. As so many of us have come to understand about tequila, it's important to learn to like the good stuff. Until the past decade or two, according to many producers, an increasingly affluent Mexican market has carted off the bulk of premium tequilas, particularly those aged in oak barrels and intended to be sipped like single-malt Scotch or a snifter of cognac. That left the generally cheaper, clear tequilas for the market north of the border, where it almost certainly made its way into margaritas, many of those made from inferior mixes. These days, everything about that process has changed dramatically, with finer tequilas finding a large U.S. fan base and even margaritas being made with fresh ingredients and considerable mixological care. For the record, the spirit known as tequila is a *mescal* (made from the cooked *piñas* of blue agave plants) from the Mexican state of Jalisco. It is generally sold as clear (*plato,* or silver, or simply *blanco*), *reposado* (literally "rested," meaning aged in barrels for two months to one year) or *añejo* (aged in barrels for a year and often more).

RED SANGRIA

RED SANGRIA

Slice peeled orange

½ ounce simple syrup
(see recipe p. 203)

4 ounces Padrillos malbec

¼ ounce Presidente brandy

Ice cubes

1 ounce Casteller Cava

Small melon balls for garnish,
if desired

Muddle the orange with the simple syrup. Add red wine and brandy and shake for 5 seconds. Pour into a wine glass with ice and top with sparkling wine. Garnish with melon balls, if desired.

WHITE SANGRIA

Ice cubes

2 ounces St. Germain Elderflower Liqueur

6 ounces Casteller Cava

Small melon balls for garnish, if desired

Fill a wine glass with ice. Pour the liqueur and sparkling wine over the ice. Stir with a straw and garnish with melon balls, if desired.

CACHACA

As if saying or spelling the wildly popular Brazilian drink *caipirinha* weren't challenging enough, the drink is made with a spirit called Cachaça (ka-shah-sah) instead of something easy like rum. Cachaça, however, is kin to the rums enjoyed elsewhere in the Americas, being distilled directly from sugar cane juice rather than from the molasses left over from sugar's refining process. In the beginning of the 17th century, the producers of sugar in various European colonies started using various byproducts to produce the alcoholic beverage which in British colonies came to be known as rum, or *tafia* in French colonies, or *aguardiente de caña* in Spanish or *aguardente da terra* in Portuguese Brazil. This last name evolved into cachaça. The actual distillation process dates back to 1532, when Portuguese colonisers brought the first cuttings of sugar cane to Brazil from Madeira, right along with the pot stills to make the magic happen. Most of today's cachaça is produced in Brazil, and most of it never leaves—something around four hundred million gallons consumed by Brazilians each year, compared with only four million gallons shared with the rest of the human race. In Brazil, cachaça is typically drunk straight or on the rocks. In most other places, it is a beloved part of tropical drinks like the *caipirinha*. The spirit is typically between 38% and 48% alcohol by volume, though a good deal of it is homemade (in the moonshine tradition) and can be any proof the still owner wants. By law, a small amount of sugar can be added.

ESPUMA DE PIÑA

6 pieces lime cut into ⅛s

1 ounce simple syrup (see recipe p. 203)

2 ounces El Jimador tequila

6 ounces pineapple juice

Ice cubes

2 sprigs fresh tarragon

Muddle lime with simple syrup, then add tequila and pineapple juice. Shake with ice and strain into a rocks glass. Garnish with tarragon sprigs.

MAYA MARTINI

Muddle orange, lime and 2 slices jalapeno in the simple syrup. Add vodka, vermouth and olive brine. Shake with ice for 10 seconds, then strain into a chilled martini glass. Garnish by floating the remaining jalapeno slice on top.

3 pieces orange cut in ⅛s

4 pieces lime cut in ⅛s

3 1 in. round slices jalapeno, seeds removed

1 ½ ounce simple syrup (see recipe p. 203)

1 ½ ounce vodka

½ ounce dry vermouth

½ ounce olive brine

Ice cubes

Pisco Sour

PISCO PUNCH

Muddle cloves with the simple syrup, then add the orange and lime and muddle again. Add the pisco and pineapple juice. Shake with ice and strain into a large pilsner glass. Finish with sparkling wine and Campari. Garnish with the orange twist.

4 whole cloves

1 ½ ounces simple syrup (see recipe p. 203)

3 pieces orange cut in ⅛s

3 pieces lime cut in ⅛s

2 ounces pisco Portón or Barsol

1 ½ ounces pineapple juice

Ice cubes

1 ounce Casteller Cava

¼ ounce Campari

Orange twist

PISCO SOUR

1 ½ ounces pisco Portón or Barsol

1 tablespoon egg white

1 ounce lime juice

1 ounce simple syrup (see recipe p. 203)

5 ice cubes

1 splash Angostura bitters

In a blender, combine all ingredients except bitters and blend until frothy, about 15 seconds. Pour into a martini glass and splash the bitters on top.

PISCO

The Pisco Sour has served as the U.S. introduction to the iconic spirit from Peru, and the story only gets more interesting from there. Pisco is technically a brandy exported primarily by Peru but also by Chile, thus producing a vigorous and ongoing cross-border "paternity suit" between the two long, tall South American nations. The stuff is made from only certain varieties of grapes, which are fermented and distilled into a potent *aguardiente*. Spanish conquistadores brought grape vines to South America, in order to make wine for their own consumption and export—as well as, of course, to help the padres celebrate the Catholic Mass. According to the yarn, pisco came into being as a way to use leftover grapes that were undesirable for winemaking. We've come across several explanations for how pisco got its name, starting with origins in the native Quechan word *piscu*, meaning a bird found in the Ica Valley of Peru. If you prefer, it may be named after the town of Pisco, a port city from which the brandy was shipped to Lima as well as popularized by sailors enjoying a night on the town. The name is also said to come from the large pre-Colombian clay pots, called *piscos*, which are actually used to ferment the grapes.

BASIC
Recipes

BEEF DEMI-GLACE

6 pounds beef bones

1 ½ pounds yellow onion, roughly chopped

¾ pound carrot, roughly chopped

¾ pound celery, roughly chopped

1 bay leaf

1 ½ cup tomato paste

2 ½ gallons plus ⅔ gallons water

3 ½ cups red wine

¾ cup all-purpose flour

¾ cup butter

1 tablespoon salt

Preheat oven to 400° F. Combine the beef bones, vegetables and bay leaf on a large baking pan and roast in oven until golden brown, about 1 hour. Transfer to a hot large braising pan or Dutch oven. Stir in the tomato paste and cook until paste turns rusty brown. Add 2 ½ gallons water and bring to a boil. Lower heat and reduce for 3 hours, then add remaining water and cook an additional 3 hours.

Remove from heat and strain through a fine sieve into a stock pot. Make a roux by combining flour and butter in a pan and cooking until sandy brown. Bring to a boil and add red wine, roux and salt. Reduce heat and simmer until liquid is reduced by ½, about 6 hours. Strain again over an ice bath to chill the demi-glace quickly. Use what you need and freeze the rest. Freezing demi-glace in small containers or even ice cube trays is a good idea, since then you can add a "cube" to anything involving meat and sauce.

CHICKEN DEMI-GLACE

Preheat broiler to 400° F. Place the chicken carcass in a roasting pan, along with the onion, leek, carrot and garlic. Season with thyme, salt and pepper. Set pan under broiler until chicken begins to turn crispy and brown. Carefully transfer the roasted chicken and vegetables to a large stock pot and add the water and tomato paste. Bring to a boil on the stovetop, then reduce heat, partially cover and cook until liquid reduces by ¾, 5-6 hours. Strain the syrupy liquid through a fine sieve. Pour into ice cube trays or other small containers and freeze for use as needed.

1 chicken carcass, split into pieces

1 onion, roughly chopped

1 leek, roughly chopped

1 carrot, roughly chopped

1 clove garlic, chopped

¼ teaspoon dried thyme leaves

¼ teaspoon salt

¼ teaspoon black pepper

1 gallon water

½ cup tomato paste

EGG WHITE MARINADE

Whisk all ingredients together in a bowl.

EGG WASH

Whisk both ingredients together until thoroughly incorporated.

PILONCILLO SIMPLE SYRUP

Combine all ingredients in a pot and bring to a boil, stirring until sugars are completely dissolved. Let cool and pour into a container. Refrigerate for use.

2 cups egg whites
½ tablespoon soy sauce
¼ cup dry sherry
1 ¾ cups cornstarch

EGG WASH
2 eggs
¼ cup milk

PILONCILLO SIMPLE SYRUP
4 cups water
4 cups granulated sugar
¼ cup piloncillo cane sugar
(available at Latin markets)

The View from HERE

I have learned to revere the culinary journeys of the past, especially as they echo and express our family's journey from Nicaragua all those years ago. Yet one thing we've learned from twenty-five years in the restaurant business is that, you really are only as good as your last meal. And that means the future. That's exciting to me. Living and cooking with the past as resource and the future as inspiration isn't a bad way to live at all.

The first food lesson I learned from my dad was the concept of the vinaigrette. Not just how to make a one to three ratio of vinegar to fat for dressing per se, but how to apply balance. The same can be said about the relationship between spicy and sweet, bitter and rich, and new and old.

In the same way the principles on flavor balance still apply, the concept of showing the versatility of the ingredients of the Americas is still exciting; it leaves a lot of room for exploration. The only thing that has changed is that Houston is now a part of our story. The influences of the cuisines of my family's hometown are now just as much a part of it as Nicaragua. For example, our family's favorite sushi spot brought about the crawfish taquito. The Mexican influence of our staff has brought things from family meal to the menu. The past is a resource, but any chef thinks in terms of what he's into 'now,' what the current is.

I often think of Latin cuisine in relationship to other ethnic foods. It's awesome that even though we are twenty-five years in business this is still emerging. Peruvian food has helped Americans see beyond the border further south, but for the most part Latin dining feels up for grabs. It's ours to write.

I learned English through Disney and MTV as a child of the 80's. At the same time, our family was mildly assimilating the food and flavors of Nicaragua into American commercial success. Our fare is and always was 'Spanglish' food. The future of our dishes will continue to reflect that. What's great is that since the American dining public is ready to embrace more micro-regional cuisines, we can incorporate more of our home cooking while still reflecting our family's experience in Texas and the U.S. A favorite Amazón dish of mine combines hotdogs with a Vigorón, a Nicaraguan street food of pickled cabbage, yuca and pork rinds.

Everything we do will be Latin in personality and foundational taste, no matter how many times we take those flavors to every corner of the globe. It's what we love, and it's who we are as a family. The good news is that Latin is considered a cuisine of immense promise in this country, much as the land itself was all those centuries ago when Europeans first started looking at it from sailing ships and lusting after its riches. Latin food, beyond a particular and

> When people taste food, they also taste culture—the long line across time filled with hopes and dreams and difficulties and mothers and fathers who make a cuisine even possible.

familiar strand of pop Tex-Mex, is still under-represented in the marketplace. Our job is to help Latin cuisine become like sushi in the '80s, Thai in the '90s or Korean right now. After all, when people taste food, they also taste culture—the long line across time filled with hopes and dreams and difficulties and mothers and fathers who make a cuisine even possible.

My Dad is the one who started this company, who created the Cordúa "brand"—a word my generation understands better than his but that he had the intuition to embrace nonetheless. He's also the one who crafted our cooking style, applying classic French techniques to the foods and food ideas of the Americas. Most of all, he was the one who taught me our mission: We're not in business to be "authentic," whatever that might mean; we're in business to be yummy. In our kitchen, nothing is sacred, and everything is fun.

The cooking of France and the rest of Europe is now in our culinary blood, as were the ingredients of my ancestors in every corner of Latin America. All of that is there for us, solid, eternal. Everything else is a blank canvas, an exciting, changing canvas on which to paint each day in the kitchen. Food, after all, is served to living men and women in a living dining room, never enshrined behind glass in some museum. It will always evolve, always change. And for me, in this same heart and soul that longed to make American movies and play American music, it will always be new.

David Cordúa

> My Dad was the one who taught me our mission: We're not in business to be "authentic," whatever that might mean; we're in business to be yummy.